I0800919

IMAGES
of America

HOLLOMAN AIR FORCE BASE

On the Cover: This aerial view of B-24 serial number 41-28571 flying southeast over Alamogordo Army Airfield was taken from the right waist position of another B-24. The large three-digit number on the nose identifies this as a training ship. This photograph was taken by Clarence E. "Hank" Schurwan Jr., an active duty US Army Air Forces photographer. (Courtesy of the 49th Wing History Office.)

IMAGES
of America

HOLLOMAN AIR FORCE BASE

Joseph T. Page II

ARCADIA
PUBLISHING

ISBN 978-0-7385-9528-3

Published by Arcadia Publishing
Charleston, South Carolina

Printed in the United States of America

Library of Congress Control Number: 2011939732

For all general information, please contact Arcadia Publishing:
Telephone 843-853-2070
Fax 843-853-0044
E-mail sales@arcadiapublishing.com
For customer service and orders:
Toll-Free 1-888-313-2665

Visit us on the Internet at www.arcadiapublishing.com

To 1st Lt. Abel R. Rojero (1979–2003). I judge myself every day against your example of an Air Force officer, but I will never come close.

Contents

ACKNOWLEDGMENTS

My acquaintance with Holloman Air Force Base is relatively recent, as my first visit to the base was in 1988. Therefore, my reliance on the experts was extremely important, and their collective wisdom and comments were invaluable. First, thanks to Darren Court of the White Sands Missile Range Museum. While we have had no formal contact, his seminal Arcadia title about the missile range demanded that a book be published about Holloman.

The vast majority of photographs used were provided by the 49th Wing Historical Archives, and unless otherwise noted, photographs appear courtesy of this source. I wish to thank members of the base's historical brain trust, the ones with the knowledge to make this project succeed. Ralph G. Jackson II, 49th Wing historian, provided a large number of photographs and his historical wisdom. J.R. Gomolak, 49th Civil Engineering Squadron, literally provided the keys to the kingdom. Thanks go out to 49th Wing commander Col. David A. Krumm, for allowing the project to go forward, to the 49th Wing Public Affairs Office for their assistance, and to Lt. Col. E. Marcus Caughey for flying top cover for all of my daily missteps. Also, T.Sgt. John Grijalva had to suffer through my writing—thanks for the thumbs up. In the community, I would like to thank the Tularosa Basin Historical Society and Jean Killer for their resources. George House, Mike Shinabery, and Michael B. Smith of the New Mexico Museum of Space History were a breath of fresh air, regaling me with space-age pictures and stories of "The Day We Almost Bombed Albuquerque."

Thanks to my editor Lauren Hummer and her even-handed approach to this project. She has been very patient answering all of my annoying questions.

Finally, thanks to my family. First, my wife, Kim, and four children. They have provided a dual purpose: providing me with a needed distraction at critical times while giving me the reasons to make this project shine. Second, thanks to my father, Joseph, and mother, Kathleen. Without them, I would not have a love of Air Force history that permeates my everyday life.

INTRODUCTION

Tucked into a small corner of the southwestern United States, Holloman Air Force Base has been at the forefront of national defense since its conceptualization in 1941. In the ramp-up of Allied assistance during World War II, the federal government began scouting sites for additional training bases. The area inside the Tularosa Basin was deemed very suitable for bombing practice and flight training with its clear skies and the low population density of its surrounding areas.

Due to a series of support and lease agreements with the British government allowing the United States to build air bases on British soil with long-term lease agreements, the US government granted reciprocal rights for training and support bases for Royal Air Force (RAF) pilots. Called the British Commonwealth Air Training Plan, the concept was utilized by members of the Commonwealth (United Kingdom, Canada, Australia, and New Zealand) to train massive numbers of aircrews in a short amount of time. One of the locations granted to "The Plan" was a parcel of land outside Alamogordo, New Mexico. However, the aftermath of December 7, 1941, forced the British to concentrate less on cross-ocean cooperation and more on operations in the European theater as well as provoking the United States to enter the war.

As the political changes following the attack on Pearl Harbor rippled through the world, the focus of the newborn training base changed from RAF pilots to American heavy bomber crews during the first six months of 1942. While the transition to training US crews was obvious, the preparation in the base's plans hinted towards deeper cooperation within the Commonwealth Air Training Plan. Any airdrop tests with a jointly developed atomic weapon would have been supported by Army Air Force bases in Albuquerque and Roswell as well as the proposed British base in Alamogordo. One major artifact that remains at Holloman from its Commonwealth Air Training Plan origins is the signature British tripartite runway pattern and cantonment plan, which has been only minimally altered.

Alamogordo Army Airfield (AAF), as the airfield was then known, fulfilled its military mission by preparing aircrews in the fine arts of bombardment, gunnery, and navigation over the Tularosa Basin. Life was as normal as could be expected on a wartime training base. Troops worked hard at their martial tasks throughout the week and then lived it up in the surrounding area with visits to the White Sands National Monument, activities in Alamogordo, and journeys to El Paso and Las Cruces. From 1942 through 1945, nineteen bombardment groups called Alamogordo AAF home, and thousands of soldiers, airmen, and support personnel trained for war on the European and Pacific fronts. But Alamogordo AAF and its contributions would have remained just a footnote in the annals of American military history if not for an obscure weapons test codenamed Trinity.

On July 16, 1945, New Mexico newspapers reported an explosion of a weapons cache located on the Alamogordo Bombing and Gunnery Range. Cities as far away as Albuquerque, Silver City, and El Paso reported broken windows and mentions of "the sun rising twice." While the War Department worked quickly to prevent any investigation into the "accidental" explosion, the truth behind the matter was more shocking—man had just entered the atomic age with the blast at 05:29:45 Mountain War Time.

After the war, the airfield was inactivated briefly, but it did not remain so long. The military's push into the atomic age demanded the increased use of missile technology. The old bombing range provided an immediately available area adjacent to the stalwart White Sands Proving Grounds. The field became the home of the Air Force's Guided Missile Test Range, a satellite field subordinate to the Air Force Missile Test Center at Patrick Air Force Base, Florida. The first rocket from the base rose into the skies of the Tularosa Basin on July 23, 1947.

A little over two months later, on September 18, the US Air Force became a separate service. Shortly after, the airfield was renamed for Col. George Vernon Holloman, a pioneer in the field of guided missiles. The base's focus was on the development of guided missile systems, and it began life as the Holloman Air Development Center before being renamed the Air Force Missile Development Center (AFMDC) in 1957.

The "Space Race" of the 1960s tapped into the lifeblood of Holloman's research. Areas as diverse as high-altitude research balloon flights, high-speed testing on a railed track, and the launching of rockets and missiles fit in neatly with the data required for manned flights into space. During the lead-up to the Apollo program, it seemed as if records were being set or broken on a weekly basis. Personnel at Holloman saw the fruits of their labor firsthand with the launches of the Mercury, Gemini, and Apollo spacecraft.

In 1970, the base was put under the aegis of Tactical Air Command (TAC), the major command responsible for all fighter aircraft in the Air Force. The 49th was the only dual-based fighter wing, with a commitment to NATO in the European theater but assets stationed at Holloman. Early in the decade, near the end of the Vietnam War, the 49th would forward-deploy most of its assets in Thailand, leaving a small garrison at Holloman to maintain the base. However, research and development in space and missile systems would continue unabated.

The late 1970s brought yet another alteration to Holloman's mission, the addition of the Tactical Training Center to the frontline fighter base. Tail code markings of "HO" were seen in the skies around the world, combining the impressive characteristics of F-15 Eagle air superiority with arguably the world's best tactical fighter pilots. Ground and air crews would continue the legacy of excellence Holloman personnel were known for by winning the 1988 William Tell Aerial Gunnery Meet. Just as in previous decades, the 1980s would end in a whimper, with the ideological struggle of the Cold War ending quickly.

The start of the 1990s would refocus Holloman's efforts yet again, this time trading large air superiority aircraft with an aircraft known for its "shadowy attack." The 49th Tactical Fighter Wing exchanged both name and aircraft in the first two years of the 1990s, becoming the 49th Fighter Wing and receiving the F-117 Nighthawk, better known to the world as the stealth fighter. Finishing out the decade, Holloman personnel would retain their elite status as home of the world's only stealth aircraft.

Challenges brought on by the new century, including the horrific attacks on September 11, 2001, only increased the wherewithal of Holloman's personnel. As some of the first responders during the Global War on Terror, their legacy has now stretched worldwide. From the mountainous regions of Afghanistan to the sandy deserts of Iraq and the cold recesses of space, fingerprints of Holloman's legacy of excellence are everywhere. And if recent history is any indication, that legacy will continue without fail into the unknown future.

One

The Premodern Era 1500–1942

The Tularosa Basin is a magnificent wonder to behold. From its raw natural beauty and stunning landmarks to the fierceness and passion of its inhabitants, it is difficult to imagine many places on Earth that offer such juxtaposition of extremes: melting heat and blistering cold, peaceful settlers and warring tribes—Native American and US military notwithstanding—and blinding sun transitioning into starkest night.

The earliest inhabitants of the basin were Mescalero Apache, who scholars believe were part Athabaskan, from the Alaskan landmass. Moving south to what is now southern New Mexico, the Mescalero held both Spanish and American interlopers at bay for more than 350 years. Only after US military campaigns in the late 1800s forced the Mescalero onto a reservation did attacks on settlers in Tularosa village and La Luz Canyon drop off dramatically.

Whites began settling the area en masse from the 1870s onward, relying on cattle to make a living. Names familiar to current residents fill out the lore of the basin: Billy the Kid, of Lincoln County War fame; the John Good and Oliver Lee feud; and the gold mining boomtown of Orogrande. When ranching returned to the Tularosa Basin after the passages of the 1916 Stock Raising Homestead Act and the Taylor Grazing Act, the ensuing federal influence was only a small taste of what was to come to the area in the next few decades.

Some ranching families, such as the McNatts, Danleys, and Boles, were instrumental in the formation of the Alamogordo Bombing and Gunnery Range and corresponding Army airfield. Ranchers' assistance, in the form of physical land and water rights, allowed the base to grow to sizable proportions during the years of World War II. In the prewar defense buildup, the federal government chose to condemn the lands within the basin for the establishment of the bombing and gunnery range, White Sands Proving Grounds, and Fort Bliss's McGregor Range for "national defense purposes." Many decades would pass before the ranchers got final resolution, which was not wholly in their favor.

A daylight view illuminates the ruins of Gran Quivira pueblo around 1915. The pueblo's ideal representation of a "lost city" filled with riches had been the focus of Francisco Coronado's journey into the Southwest during the early 1500s. Coronado never found his "Cities of Gold" but discovered much about the Native American tribes that inhabited the Plains. His journey was the first—but not the last—through these lands. (Photograph by O.E. Meinzer, courtesy of US Geologic Survey.)

This photograph, taken around 1915 from the eastern edge of the Tularosa Basin facing west, deftly displays the San Andreas mountain range north of Las Cruces. On April 6, 1880, US 9th Cavalry "Buffalo Soldiers" drove Mescalero Apaches, led by Chief Victorio, out of the San Andreas. In the foreground, what is now known as Tulie Peak juts up from the desert floor, prominently disturbing the otherwise flat landscape. (Photograph by O.E. Meinzer, courtesy of US Geologic Survey.)

A salt creek flows through the Tularosa Basin around 1915. Historically, the climate in the basin is arid, with less than 10 inches of precipitation collecting. Summer months are considered monsoon season by residents. The geographic layout of the basin shields the majority of desert land from precipitation common in the upper elevations of the surrounding Sacramento Mountains. (Photograph by O.E. Meinzer, courtesy of US Geologic Survey.)

Travelers stop by a groundwater pond around 1915. The pond was created by a sinkhole from the underground streams common in the basin. As early as 1869, residents realized underground streams ran through the subsurface. One particular water flow was named the "Lost River," flowing at a minimum depth of three feet but going as deep as 50 feet in some locations. (Photograph by O.E. Meinzer, courtesy of US Geologic Survey.)

Gypsum sand is intermixed with scrub brush and salt marsh on the eastern end of the Tularosa Basin. Gypsum deposits were created by the ancient lakes in the area, which engulfed the entire basin during the Pleistocene era. The deposits were eventually worn down into sand grains and moved by wind activity in the intervening millennia. (Photograph by O.E. Meinzer, courtesy of US Geologic Survey.)

A lone individual poses within "Soda Lake" around 1915. The gypsum deposits continued to accumulate through the constant re-creation cycle of Lake Lucero, located within the Tularosa Basin. White Sand National Monument was created from 224 square miles of gypsum in the 1930s. The following decades would find the majority of the monument used as a military testing area within the White Sands Missile Range. (Photograph by O.E. Meinzer, courtesy of US Geologic Survey.)

Luther Boles, a veteran of World War I, built his residence and farm west of the Sacramento Mountains. The Army Air Corps, and later the US Air Force, contracted Boles's land to provide a lifeline of water to the expanding base in the late 1940s and early 1950s. Boles retained use of his land until 1954, when the Air Force began condemnation proceedings. (Courtesy of the US Army Corps of Engineers Albuquerque Office.)

Doug McNatt sits on Old Headlight at McNatt Ranch. The vehicle in the background displays an early example of a New Mexico license plate, with a conspicuously placed Zia symbol on the left side of the plate. The symbol's inclusion and the darkened color of the plate dates the photograph to the late 1920s or early 1930s. (Photograph by Susie McNatt, courtesy of the 49th Wing History Office.)

Joe, Tommy, and Carr McNatt (from left to right) pose together at the McNatt Ranch in 1935. Their legacy, the family ranch, was taken by the federal government for the bombing range in January 1942. After losing the ranch, their father, Doug McNatt, took a construction job helping to build the first facilities on the air base. C.C. McNatt died in 1950 and Doug in 1980, and they never regained ownership of their land. (Photograph by Susie McNatt, courtesy of the 49th Wing History Office.)

From left to right, Doug McNatt, Buck Sellars, and Wayne and Bill McCommis repair the corral fencing at "Old Home Place" around 1926. McNatt is holding the fence post, while Sellars is handing him wire pliers. The Old Home Place location in Malone Draw was popular with settlers, with several potential homesteaders filing for ownership with the state of New Mexico. Permanent settlement began with C.C. McNatt's purchase of the tract. (Photograph by Susie McNatt, courtesy of the 49th Wing History Office.)

From left to right, Tommy McNatt rides Patches, Joe McNatt rides Pal, and C.C. McNatt follows on an unnamed horse at the McNatt Ranch in the early 1930s. The ranch site encompassed more than 50,000 square meters and included two houses, a windmill, water storage tanks, livestock pens and corral, a granary, and workshop buildings. (Photograph by Susie McNatt, courtesy of the 49th Wing History Office.)

Christopher Columbus McNatt, known as "Lum" or "C.C.," rides his horse in the late 1940s. Born on March 20, 1871, in Arkansas, he grew up in the Upper Penasco area of the Sacramento Mountains. C.C. and his wife, Ella, moved to Alamogordo in 1911 to aid in their children's schooling and to ease Ella's declining health. (Photograph by Susie McNatt, courtesy of the 49th Wing History Office.)

Doug McNatt, standing on the fence to the right, is helping to break horses at the Old Home Place. Doug McNatt and his wife, Susie, lived temporarily at the Old Home Place with Doug's parents, C.C. and Ella McNatt, for two years. Afterwards, they relocated to a new homestead farther south to escape the floodwaters common in the Malone Draw area. (Photograph by Susie McNatt, courtesy of the 49th Wing History Office.)

Tommy Danley, nearly two years old, is shown here playing at the Old Home Place on November 18, 1939. Osie Danley and his wife, Garnie, improved the homestead by adding a one-room house, a privy, a chicken house, windmills, horse corrals, and a milk pen. The farm also included a small herd of cattle, a milk cow, chickens, and a couple of hogs. (Photograph by Tommy Danley, courtesy of the 49th Wing History Office.)

Tommy Danley sits on the porch of the Danley house at the Old Home Place before his first birthday. Born on January 18, 1938, to Osie and Garnie Danley, Tommy was only four years old when the federal government confiscated the family's land for the air base and bombing range. He continued to live in the area, raising three sons and running a local paving business. (Photograph by Tommy Danley, courtesy of the 49th Wing History Office.)

In this photograph, Green family cattle are driven down the Sacramento Mountains to winter pasture. Driving cattle down the mountain, sometimes to railroad stock pens, was a regular occurrence between Alamogordo and El Paso. Current residents of the area ride Highway 82, following the reverse path up the mountain to the village of Cloudcroft. (Photograph by Carrie Green, courtesy of the 49th Wing History Office.)

The Danley family poses in front of the valuable corn crop at their ranch. They are, from left to right, (first row) Lela Danley, Gene Danley, and Dave Danley; (second row) Maggie Danley (holding Jewell Danley's daughter Shirley), Claude Danley, Jack Danley, and Ruby Danley (Maggie's sister). The corn in the background was grown with the help of the floodwaters common in low-lying parts of the Tularosa Basin, such as Malone Draw. (Photograph by Willis Danley, courtesy of the 49th Wing History Office.)

During happier times, Garnie, Osie, and Tommy Danley pose at their ranch. Osie understood the revocation of his ranchland for national security reasons during the years of World War II. Later, however, the family and its descendants would continue to petition the federal government in court for the deeds to their land. (Photograph by Tommy Danley, courtesy of the 49th Wing History Office.)

Two

Alamogordo Army Airfield 1942–1947

After the abandonment of the British Overseas Training Base plan by the US government, Alamogordo Army Airfield opened to little fanfare in the summer of 1942. The war was on, and American towns all over the country were supporting the war effort by hosting Army training posts. The Tularosa Basin was fortunate enough to have the low population, beautiful flying weather, and spacious desert required for bombardment training. The dual-theater war required the use of many types of bombardment aircraft flown by crews of up to 10 men. The various combat airframes had a few things in common: high capacity for carrying bombs, bristling machine guns for self-protection, and highly trained aircrews versed in complex tasks such as navigation. Alamogordo Bombing and Gunnery Range provided the means to train all three—spacious skies, featureless deserts, and mountainous terrain for varied navigation tasks; shrubs and cacti waiting to explode from anxious bombardiers' properly placed weapons; and Jeeps-on-rails awaiting demise from a gunner's hot lead.

Flying officially began when the 301st Bombardment Group arrived on May 27, 1942. The B-17s arrived a month later. The aircraft flown at Alamogordo Army Airfield showed off the power and variety of the American military machine: B-17 Flying Fortresses, B-24 Liberators, P-47 Thunderbolts, and B-29 Superfortresses. Nineteen bombardment groups and one fighter group made the basin their temporary home at various times during the three war years (1942–1945).

While the excitement of fighter tactics frequently steals the public's imagination, there is little dispute that heavy bombardment won the war. As bomber pilots are so fond of saying, "Fighter pilots make movies; bomber pilots make history!" Truer words have rarely been spoken. In addition, B-29 Superfortress crews trained at Alamogordo AAF's southern location while the testing of the first atomic weapon was taking place on the far northern end of the range.

This aerial view of Alamogordo Army Airbase faces toward the northwest of the Tularosa Basin. The British-derived tripartite runway is visible as a giant "X," with the third runway, across the length of the photograph, connecting the two legs of the cross. Present-day Highway 70 is visible in the lower third of the photograph, creating a "T" junction with the main entry road to the air base.

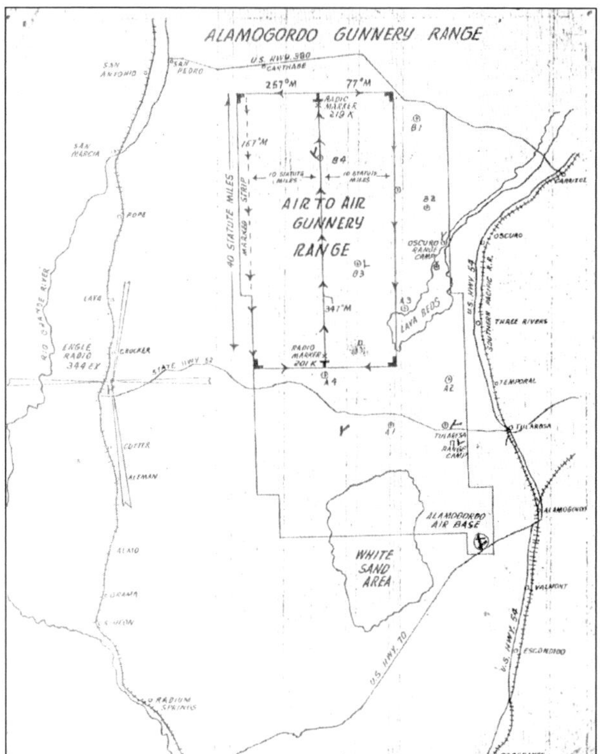

This early-1940s map outlines the Alamogordo Gunnery and Bombing Range. The aircraft bombing range stretched throughout the Tularosa Basin but left the commercial traffic route on Highway 52. When White Sands Proving Grounds took over the remainder of the basin, the spur of 52 traveling through the San Andres Mountains was closed to commercial traffic.

A B-24 Liberator flies westward over the White Sands National Monument. Existing images of Air Force aircraft flying inside the United States (or "ZI," Zone of Interior) are rare due to the intense security restrictions placed upon personnel during World War II. Fortunately, enough AAF personnel violated these rules to provide wonderful images from this era.

Hangar 301 releases a "beast of the air." Throughout the intervening decades, Hangar 301 would see the B-29, which dropped the atomic bomb, also drop thousands of missiles, unmanned drones, and fighter aircraft of both German and American origin. Today, Hangar 301 still houses the high-tech aircraft that give the US Air Force its technological edge.

The 359th Headquarters Unit took command of the Alamogordo AAF in early 1942, a year before this photograph of the headquarters echelon was taken. The day-to-day functions covered by the headquarters echelon allowed the bombardment groups to concentrate on training for combat instead of housekeeping chores. This was important, because bombardment squadrons often rotated out within weeks of their arrival in New Mexico.

An Army Air Force instructor shows students how a top gunner sits during an attack run. Bombardment aircraft in the World War II era did not have the luxury of fighter escorts, so each aircraft became a "flying fortress," furnishing protective guns on all sides. The majority of the crew for a typical aircraft focused solely on defensive measures.

Aircrew members check the mission schedule board before flying a training sortie. Similar pre-mission planning briefs have remained constant through to the modern era of air warfare. The schedule was tight, as denoted by the sequential mission numbers and aircraft numbers. Even with plenty of airframes and crews, ramp parking and allotted times by air traffic control remain the limiting factors for any air operation. (Courtesy of the Tularosa Basin Historical Society.)

A bombardier practices on a bombing run. The bombardier's main weapon, aside from the aircraft's bombs, was the Norden bombsight. Created by Swiss émigré Carl Norden, the bombsight allowed circular-error probable accuracies of 75 feet, an amazing feat for that era's technology. The bombardier's sight also allowed minimal control over the aircraft during a bomb run in order to rapidly respond without directly involving the pilot or copilot.

A classroom instructor covers low-altitude bombing techniques for new aircrews. The primary purpose of Alamogordo AAF was to train aircrews, so this meant classroom time, and lots of it. Since most units stayed together before shipping out, all crews had the same level of knowledge and training before heading off to Europe. Bombing runs and gunnery practice on the Jeep track kept skills sharp. (Courtesy of the Tularosa Basin Historical Society.)

B-24 Liberators fly westward over the Tularosa Basin. The B-24 was by far the most common airframe located at Alamogordo AAF, with 10 bombardment groups calling the basin home throughout the early 1940s. While they only remained at the base for a short time, the wide-open spaces of the New Mexico desert allowed crews to hone their finely crafted bombardment skills.

Masons work on creating the base oven for the mess hall. The mess facilities at Alamogordo AAF were a bit primitive, even by 1940s standards. But the base housed 19 different bombardment groups during the war years, with each group usually including three squadrons of at least 40 men. When support personnel are factored in as well, it is easy to see why large "primitive" ovens were necessary.

The day room of an unidentified squadron at Alamogordo AAF sits unoccupied during training hours. Day rooms, common to almost any branch of service, were communal areas for rest, relaxation, mission planning, and any number of other activities. If the units remained at a particular garrison for a long period of time, the day room would be decorated with trophies and other knick-knacks from unit members.

Two aircrew members discuss an upcoming mission with their flying instructor, at the far right. The relative youthfulness of both the crewmembers and the instructor was common during the World War II era. The average age of a US Army Air Force aircrew member was 26.

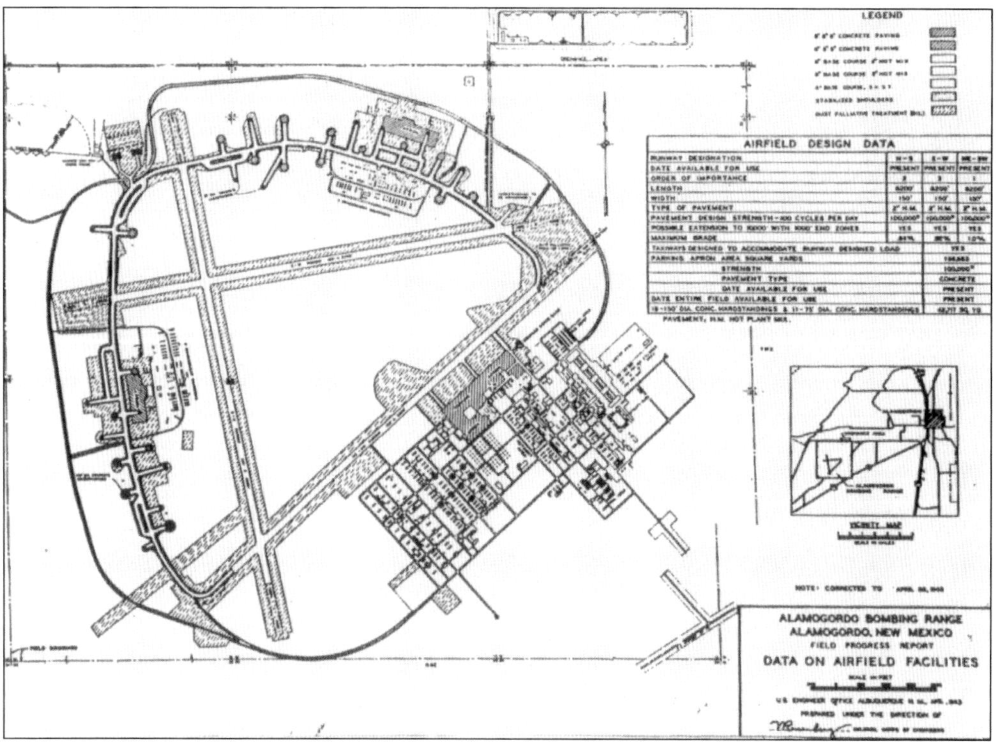

This airfield design data from the Army Corps of Engineers, Albuquerque Office, is dated 1943. The distinctive airfield design is seen, along with a vicinity map in the lower right. All the runways were equal in length, at 8,200 feet. Very little has been fundamentally changed from this original plan in the base's 70 years of service to the nation.

This photograph shows a typical New Mexico afternoon, with clear skies and clouds rolling over the Sacramento Mountains. The ramp, here covered in B-24 Liberators, is still there and is the home of Holloman's US Army Aviation contingent and the 46th Test Group. A current-day view of the parking ramp would find remote-controlled F-4 Phantoms II, ready to fly over the testing range. (Courtesy of the Tularosa Basin Historical Society.)

Three crewmembers fill out mission reports. The black shading around the right eye of each individual was formed by looking through a bombsight eyepiece for long periods of time. The Norden bombsight was the standard equipment used by Army Air Forces on almost every bombardment aircraft flown in World War II, though it is unknown whether the Norden would cause this type of impression. (Courtesy of the Tularosa Basin Historical Society.)

In this photograph of the inside of a typical enlisted member's quarters in the mid-1940s, the jury-rigged oven, which provided heat, is seen to the right. Storage space (at left) was minimal but more than troops would see in a warzone. (Courtesy of Tularosa Basin Historical Society.)

The housing section on the air base was known as "Black Housing," due to the black tar paper on the outside walls and roof. These structures, typical of the mid-1940s, were nothing more than lumber and tar paper held together by nails.

Three

"We Develop Missiles, Not Air!" 1948–1970

After surviving the threat of defense cutbacks following the post–World War II military downsizing, the base obtained two prominent features that stayed constant for the next 65 years: a new name and a leadership role in developing missile systems for the US military. The base name was altered slightly after the creation of a separate Air Force in 1947 into Alamogordo Air Force Base before finally becoming Holloman Air Force Base in January 1948. The name recognized the accomplishments of Col. George Vernon Holloman, an early pioneer in the development of guided missile systems, who died in an airplane crash in Formosa in 1946.

"We Develop Missiles, not Air," was a very bold statement made by Maj. Gen. Leighton Ira Davis during the renaming ceremony changing the Holloman Air Development Center into the Air Force Missile Development Center. The new name more appropriately reflected the base's primary concentration: missile-related activities and cutting-edge space research. The boon to the base was immense—Holloman was no longer identified alongside "other" Air Development Centers within Air Force Systems Command. Raising the center's profile as a service-level asset—as part of the integrated White Sands Missile Range—helped it gain more work on Cold War–era defense systems.

High-priority projects at Holloman during this time included the TM-61 Matador and TM-76 Mace nuclear-tipped tactical cruise missiles, the SM-62 Snark intercontinental cruise missile, and construction work lengthening the base's already impressive high-speed test track from 5,000 feet to 35,000 feet. Work continued in other aspects of space research as well, with more manned balloon flights in Projects Excelsior and Stargazer following the information gleaned from early manned and unmanned programs like Manhigh and Moby Dick. Finally, contributions to the civil space program came in the form of training simians— rhesus monkeys and chimpanzees—to see if man's closest evolutionary cousins could perform complex tasks in a hostile environment such as outer space.

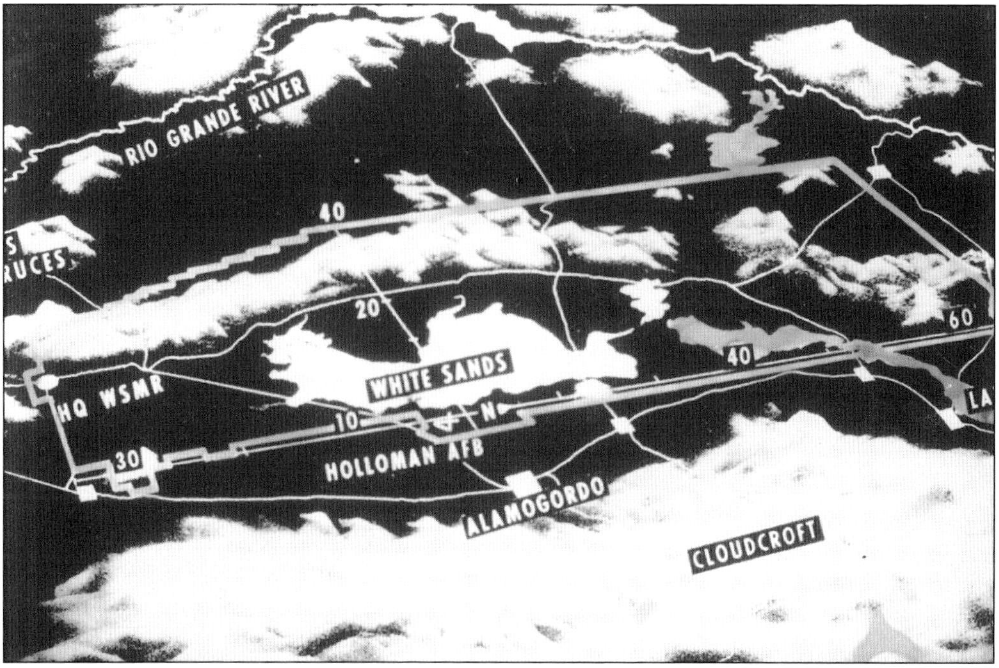

Graphic depictions of Tularosa Basin usually included the land taken up by White Sands Missile Range and Holloman Air Force Base. However, the southern extension into West Texas by Fort Bliss was not usually acknowledged. When needed, extensible range conditions would encompass all three military bases for testing purposes. In the 1980s and 1990s, exercises such as Roving Sands would take place throughout the basin.

Indicative of a different time in American culture, Holloman Air Development Center personnel had holiday greeting postcards created for distribution. The HADC moniker lasted about a decade, so this card dates from 1952 to 1957, when the center was renamed Air Force Missile Development Center. The center rocket was of ambiguous design, representing many of the launch vehicles tested on the base's grounds.

This photograph of a reconstructed V-2 rocket lifting off from White Sands Proving Ground in 1946 is autographed by Dr. Ernst Steinhoff, Kurt Lindner, Gerd W. de Beek, Hans Gruene, Werner Kuers, and Heins Millinger, German members of Operation Paperclip, who remained part of the Holloman community until a mass exodus to other locations lessened their numbers. (Courtesy of the New Mexico Museum of Space History.)

This concrete blockhouse, known as Building 1139, held the command and control functions for the Ground-to-Air Pilotless Aircraft (GAPA) program. The building provided support for many other programs from its construction date in 1947 until missile testing at Holloman ended in the late 1950s. The walls of the two-room blockhouse are two feet thick and made of reinforced concrete, while the roof held a maximum thickness of six feet of concrete.

An American copy of the V-1 "Buzz Bomb," this JB-2 (Jet Bomb) Loon is readied for launch in May 1948. The cylindrical tube on top of the winged fuselage is the jet engine. The Germans had launched thousands of V-1s from northern France and Holland aimed at London in 1944. Around the same time, American JB-2s were starting development, modeled on a captured V-1 provided by the British. (Courtesy of New Mexico Museum of Space History.)

Robert Montgomery (foreground) and William Cox (background) tweak the instrument timing system of the MX-770 in the North American Test Instrumentation Vehicle (NATIV) blockhouse during a launch in 1948. NATIV was a short-lived program, lasting only 20 flights, but it eliminated the use of rocket engines for cruise propulsion, forcing reliance on turbojets and ramjets. (Courtesy of New Mexico Museum of Space History.)

The raison d'etre for the Holloman High Speed Test Track, the SM-62 Snark, sits on the 35,000-foot test track in 1950. The Snark was the Air Force's only intercontinental cruise missile, relying on thrust propulsion after a high-altitude cruise to reach its target. The missiles were active for a brief time and only at Presque Isle Air Force Base in Maine.

German schoolchildren pose for a class portrait at Fort Bliss, Texas, in 1946. When US forces in Europe enacted Operation Paperclip to recover missile parts, blueprints, and experts from the remnants of the German military, the experts' family members were also included. These students would disperse throughout the Southwest, calling Fort Bliss, White Sands Proving Grounds, and Holloman Air Force Base home.

Paperclip children fill this one-room schoolhouse in 1946. The legacy of the German culture has remained constant since the end of World War II in the Tularosa Basin. Even during the exodus of Werner von Braun's contingent to NASA and Huntsville, Alabama, some German scientists and engineers remained behind at Holloman to continue their research.

Don Layne stands in front of a refurbished Culver PQ-14 Cadet drone in 1949. Layne purchased the aircraft from salvage from Holloman Air Force Base and restored it to pre-drone configuration. Used during World War II, the PQ-14s were beloved by crew chiefs for their maintainability and trouble-free operation. Most PQ-14s were blasted out of the sky during gun training, but a handful of them still survive today.

In the aftermath of a successful missile test, this QB-17 drone displays a shredded tail courtesy of a prototype AIM-4 missile. Surplus B-17 Flying Fortresses were converted to radio-controlled targets in the postwar rush, with 107 of them flying—and dying—over Air Research and Development Command ranges from coast to coast.

This polyethylene balloon is inflated for Project Moby Dick on June 3, 1952. The winch near the bottom of the balloon allows for the material to inflate without getting knots or other deformities in the bag. Moby Dick was reported in the press as a project studying the high-altitude, near-space environment. Its real purpose, however, was more in line with Cold War national security priorities.

A Project Moby Dick balloon is extended from its carrier wagon during inflation. As a robust intelligence collection system, Moby Dick was a failure. However, some system components lived on in another national security intelligence collection system. Run by the National Reconnaissance Office, the Corona satellite utilized a similar pickup system with a specially outfitted C-119 to snatch film capsules from the air.

This photograph shows a Project Moby Dick balloon during inflation. The covered wagon proved to be a highly satisfactory launch platform. With the wagon, balloons were launched in winds about three times as strong (20–25 knots) as they would on a platform launching with a simple hold-down system. The latter combination only provided adequate facilities for launchings in winds up to eight knots.

A Project Moby Dick balloon is inflated while inside a covered wagon. The covered wagon was built to allow the inflating and launching of large Moby Dick plastic balloons in adverse weather conditions. It employed a flatbed as a base, with a headboard and side framework constructed of canvas-covered pipe and angle iron.

Preparations are made for a Project Moby Dick flight on June 4, 1952. The real purpose of Moby Dick was to fly high-altitude cameras over Soviet territory during the early days of the Cold War. The cameras with exposed film would then be plucked from the sky by a C-119 Flying Boxcar and taken by the intelligence community for processing.

This is an excellent shot of an MX-776 Radar Scanning Link (RASCAL) air-to-surface missile. Later designated the GAM-63 (Ground-to-Air Missile), the RASCAL was the first strategic missile deployed on US aircraft. Wanting to give World War II–era bombers nuclear standoff attack capability, the RASCAL was essentially a V-2 launched horizontally off an aircraft. RASCAL was not in inventory long, first deployed in 1957 and removed from service in 1959.

A B-29B-60-BA Superfortress, serial number 44-84073, performs a takeoff sequence with jet-assisted rocket bottles due to extra weight on October 23, 1951. This particular aircraft was used as a mothership for X-7/XQ-5 programs at Holloman Air Force Base and continued its service until January 28, 1954, when it was sent to Burbank, California, and disposed of.

A remotely piloted OQ-19 drone is tweaked by two technicians right before launch. The OQ-19 was a four-cylinder radio-controlled vehicle with a maximum speed of 185 miles per hour. The maximum ceiling for the drone was between 5,000 and 10,000 feet, the right altitude for early air defense weapons.

An unidentified B-29 mothership carrier drops a Q-2 Firebee subsonic drone over the gypsum dunes of White Sands National Monument during the 1950s. Early Q-2 Firebee drones were only subsonic, allowing fighters of the day to catch up to and overtake targets. Later Firebees were supersonic and also expanded the testing envelope to air defense missile intercepts.

An F-89B is towed to a ground launch site at the North American Aviation area. This was a "tie-down" test of the Falcon missile from the F-89B's wing pods.

This image captures the underbelly view of a B-50 in captive flight of a MX-776 RASCAL missile.

In a scene reminiscent of Lt. Col. John P. Stapp's record-breaking ride, actor John Hodiak (left) is examined by Guy Madison and Dean Jagger (center) at the conclusion of a rocket sled test ride in a scene from *On the Threshold of Space*. Unstrapping Hodiak is Jake Superata, the rocket sled mechanic from Northrop Aircraft who performed the same function in Colonel Stapp's real-life rides.

Lt. Albert V. Zaborowski adjusts skin-diving equipment on a 134-pound anthropomorphic dummy. The dummy and equipment were submerged inside of a water-filled capsule and hurled along the 35,000-foot high-speed test track to determine the effects of a water-cushioned impact.

Lt. Col. John P. Stapp's rocket test sled comes screaming to a halt during a run at the high-speed test track in December 1954. The test track filled sections in the middle and on the sides of the track with water to slow down the test sleds from near-Mach speeds to zero within seconds.

Lt. Col. John P. Stapp and Col. M. Sweeney pose at the 1955 Rocket Society banquet in Alamogordo. During his time at Holloman, Lieutenant Colonel Stapp noted that the military lost as many men to fatal automobile accidents as were lost during plane crashes. Using the test track, Stapp studied car crashes by putting dummies into salvaged automobiles and projecting them into wood and concrete barriers.

Continuing his research into high-altitude environments, Capt. Joseph W. Kittinger II, sits inside a C-130 Hercules aircraft preparing for a "low altitude" jump of 28,000 feet. Captain Kittinger's assignment to the Aerospace Medical Laboratory, part of the Wright Air Development Center, in Dayton, Ohio, allowed him to take part in the record-setting activities. Kittinger later flew in combat and survived 11 months in a Vietnamese prison.

Capt. Joseph W. Kittinger II watches patiently as the two-million-cubic-foot polyethylene balloon receives its first partial inflation on November 16, 1959. This jump, Excelsior I, would be listed as the highest altitude reached by a man in an open balloon: 76,400 feet. Kittinger took 14 minutes to reach the ground after a three-minute freefall took him down to 12,000 feet and a parachute brought him gently to the ground. This was the first test of a six-foot stabilizing parachute, designed to reduce tumbling and spinning. Kittinger made another attempt only three weeks later on December 11.

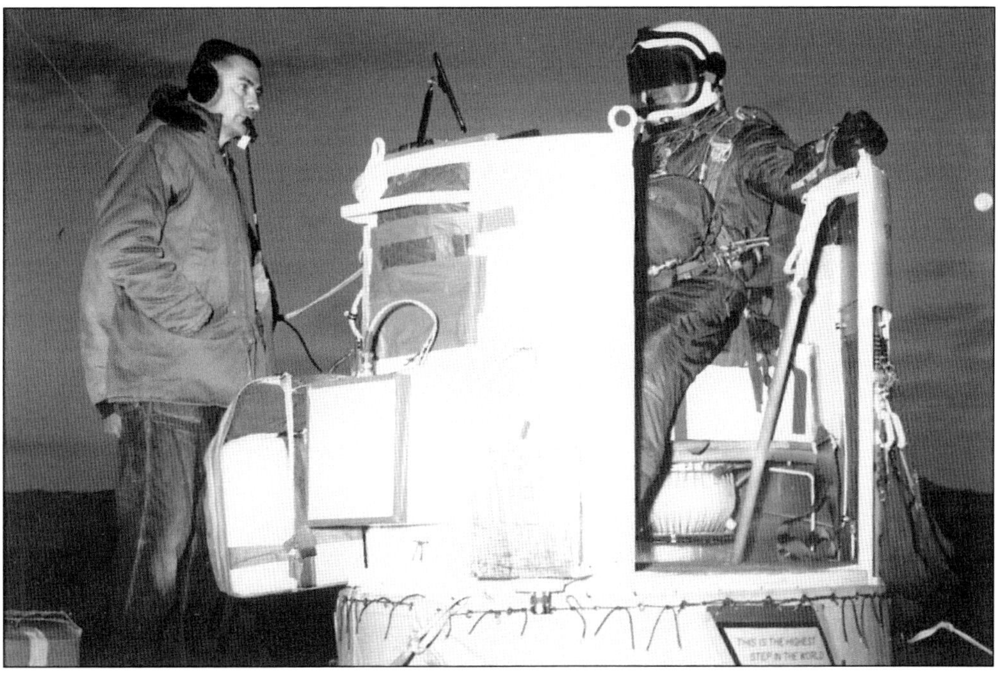

Captain Kittinger, sitting atop the Project Excelsior gondola, is observed by two technicians. The gondola was open to the environment, requiring Kittinger to use a pressure suit. The jumps tested the Beaupre parachute system, developed by an engineer at Wright Air Development Center for high-altitude ejections. Until Kittinger's tests, it was believed unlikely that aircrews could survive high-altitude egress.

Conferring with a test technician, Captain Kittinger prepares for his December 11, 1959, flight. After the jump carried him 74,700 feet in the air, he did a free-fall parachute drop of 55,000 feet over three minutes and 40 seconds followed by a regular parachute ride at 17,500 feet to a soft landing near the White Sands National Monument.

Captain Kittinger is helped out of his gear by two ground personnel after his record-breaking November jump of 76,400 feet.

Technicians inspect the inside of the Project Stargazer gondola in November 1962, preparing for Captain Kittinger's December flight. The gondola was originally designed as a platform for a high-altitude escape program, but since the gondola was unneeded at the time, the 13-foot-high cylinder was modified into a manned configuration for scientific research in 1958.

Sally Simons beams at the camera, wearing her famous father's test helmet. Dr. (Maj.) David Simons took a Manhigh balloon gondola to a record-breaking height of 101,516 feet—or about 20 miles above the Earth—on August 19–20, 1957. His 32-hour flight was a boon for research scientists, as he performed 25 different experiments during flight, from observing the moon and Venus to recording cosmic ray bombardment on his body.

A peek into this modern-looking pediatric facility assures that the health and welfare of these baby chimpanzees are well taken care of by the 6571st Aeromedical Research Lab at Holloman. Chimpanzee babies Phyllis (left) and Little "K" (standing) romp around in the playpen, while Josephine, born prematurely, sleeps peacefully in the incubator.

This aerial photograph from the early 1960s shows the Holloman Aeromedical Primate Facility. As the manned Space Race continued through the 1960s and 1970s, the primates were needed less for testing. The Air Force closed its primate research facility in 1998 and transferred the chimpanzees to a private research foundation. A primate facility run by the National Institutes of Health is still present on Holloman grounds.

Enos, the second Project Mercury chimpanzee sent into space, sits on a training device at the Holloman Air Force Base primate facility. Enos's flight on November 29, 1961, preceded the Mercury astronauts' first orbital launch. He rode an amazing 183 minutes in weightlessness to an orbital height of 146 miles at apogee. After his return to Earth, Enos lived for another year, but he died suddenly in November 1962. (Courtesy of the New Mexico Museum of Space History.)

A talented chimpanzee at the Aeromedical Research Laboratory concentrates on selecting the correct matching symbol in a test devised to train tasks performed in space. The chimps at the facility were also taught how to count, operate push-buttons and levers, respond to light and sound stimuli, and perform other tasks related to biomedical space research studies.

A geodetic control marker for White Sands Proving Grounds is prominently displayed. The merging of the Holloman Air Force Base and White Sands Missile Range into a National Test Range took place in 1952. Throughout the intervening decades, the dual-service relationship has remained strong, with Holloman providing air traffic control and other airspace duties for the range and White Sands Range Control monitoring tests and other activities.

This directional sign pointed towards the ABLE 51 launch site. The BQM-34A nomenclature used on the sign dates it to 1963 or later, as prior to the 1963 Tri-Service Aircraft Designation System, the drone was known as the Q-2. ABLE 51 also contained a unique launch method developed for fighter aircraft known as ZEro Length (ZEL). Using a rocket motor, an F-100 Super Sabre could be airborne at 300 miles per hour in six seconds.

Three young chimpanzees play inside the Holloman Aeromedical Research Laboratory's primate facility. The laboratory was an applied research site and part of the Air Force Systems Command's Aerospace Medical Division. Two famous primate space travelers drew their names from this division: HAM (Holloman AeroMedical) and SAM (School of Aerospace Medicine).

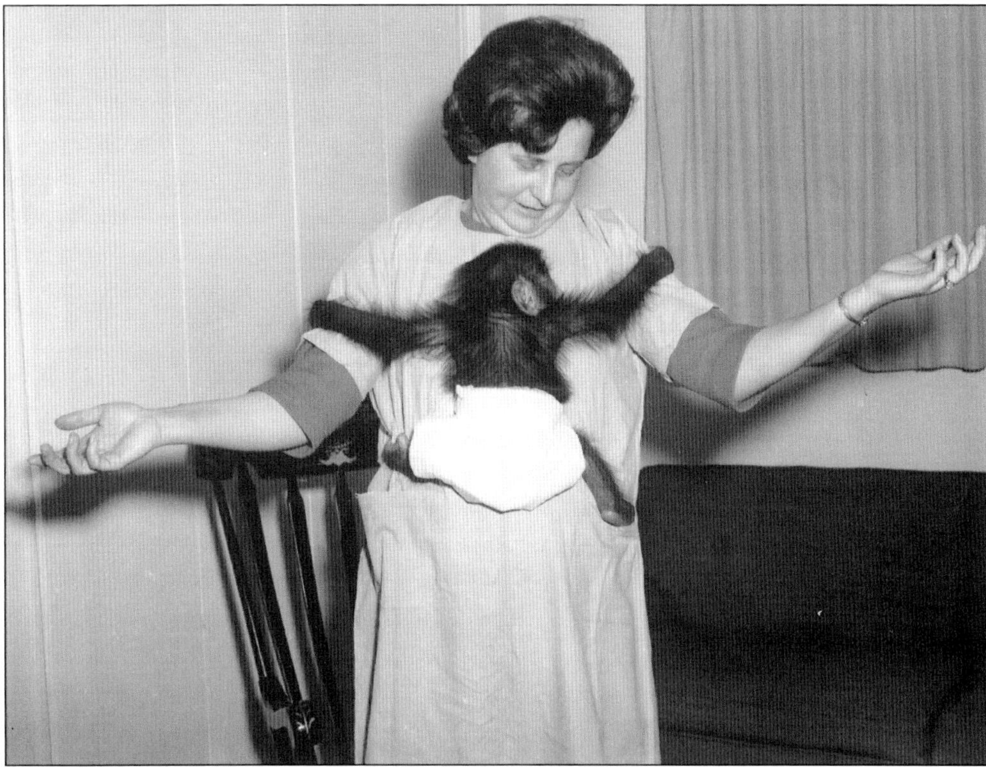

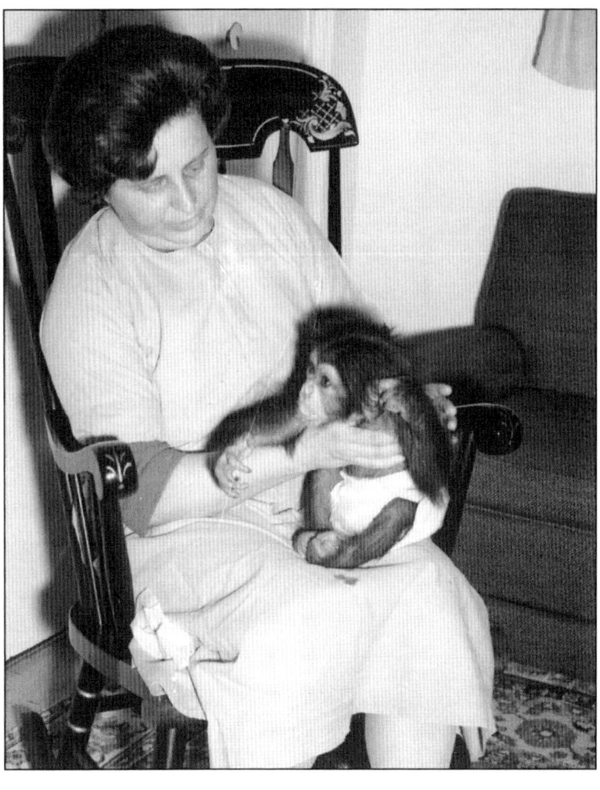

Six-week-old Phyllis demonstrates the amazing strength of a baby chimpanzee by clinging tightly to Janice Kratochvil, the wife of Col. Clyde Kratochvil, MD, director of the 6571st Aeromedical Research Laboratory (ARL). Baby chimpanzees were raised in the animal research portion of the Holloman Aeromedical Center, known as the "Holloman Zoo."

Janice Kratochvil, shown here cuddling and rocking Phyllis, taught the "art" of rocking and burping baby chimpanzees to ARL Air Force men at the labs.

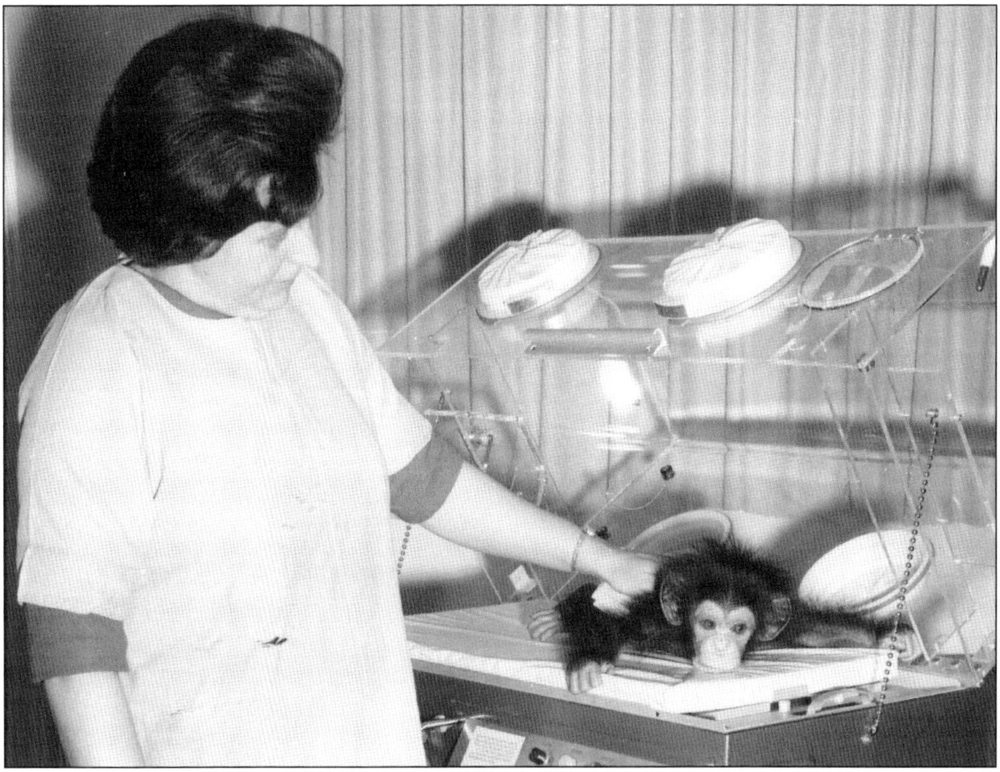

This baby chimp was kept in an incubator in the Kratochvil home for six weeks until transfer to the lab.

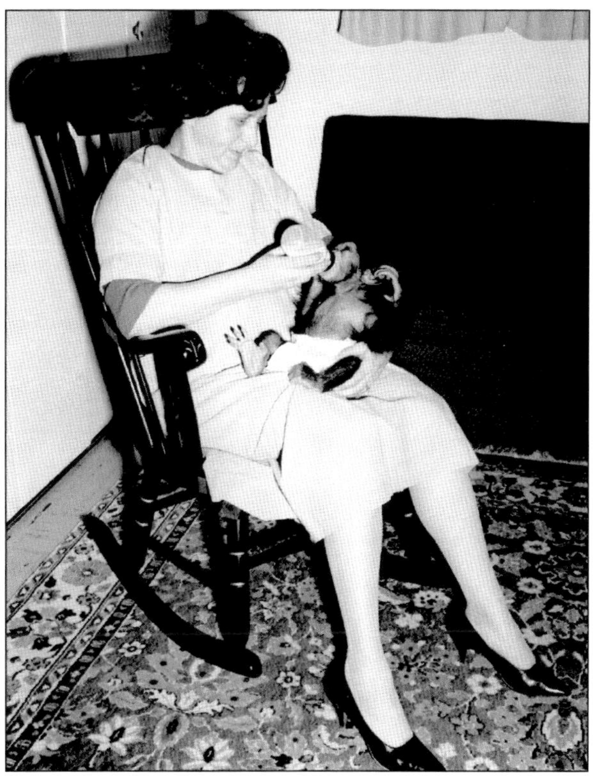

Phyllis the chimp was fed standard human-baby formula. After caring for her own five human babies, Janice Kratochvil stated ruefully, "You forget how rough those 2:00 a.m. feedings can be."

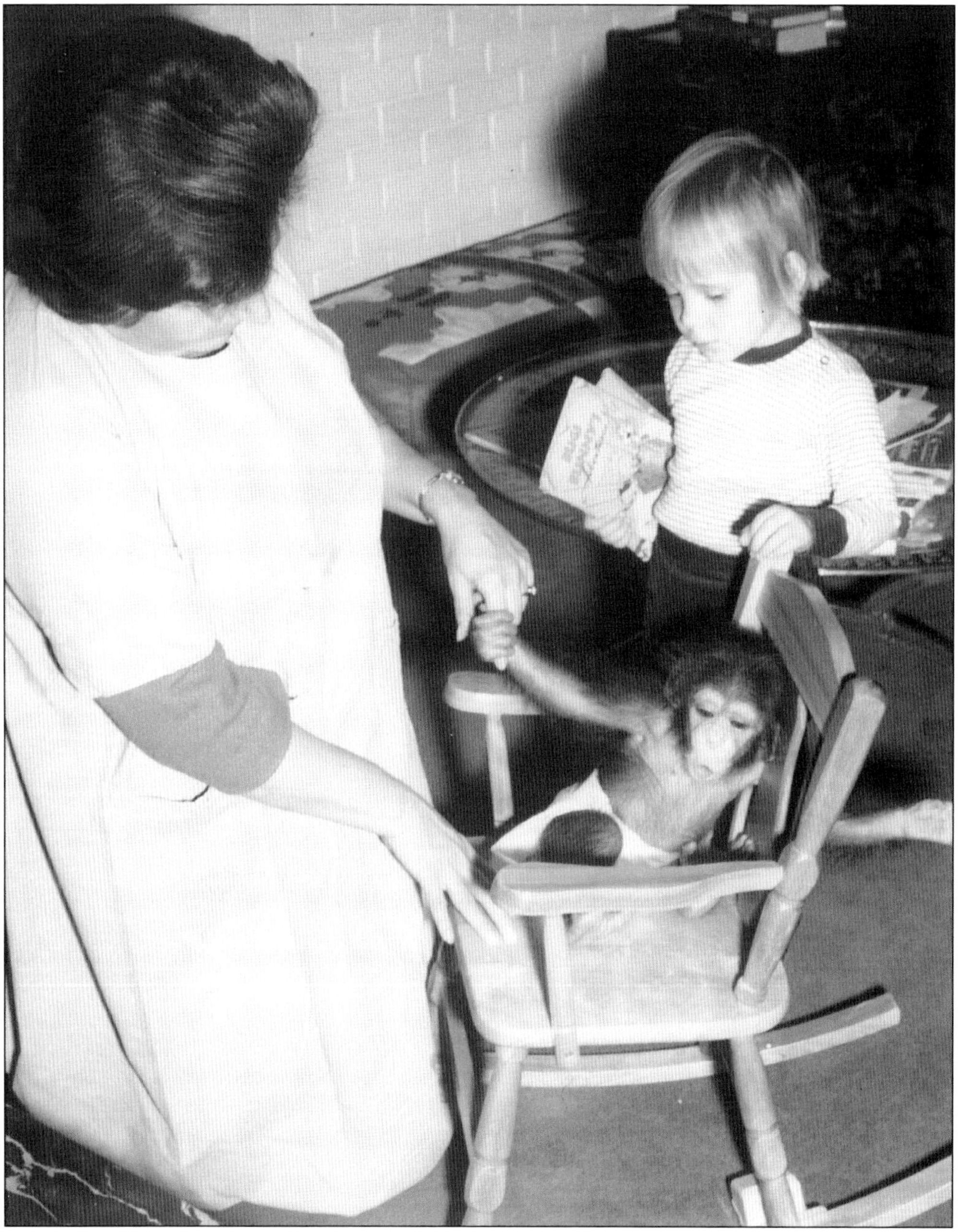

Colonel and Janice Kratochvil's three-year-old daughter Mimi graciously shares her rocking chair with Phyllis. However, the baby chimp made it quite clear that she preferred lap rocking to the do-it-yourself chair.

Harlan Sluyter Jr. (right) and an unnamed colleague help a high-speed track survey team during a test run. During the 1950s and 1960s, the local community held the base's rocket and missile research in high esteem. In the early 1960s, a section of the American Rocket Society was based at Holloman, with a few hundred members, but by the beginning of the 1970s, the section had folded.

At Armed Forces Day in 1961, free transportation for "small fries" rolls along the flight line. A steely-eyed airman second class from the aircraft maintenance division plays the role of the "engine" conductor. Air shows and open houses are good opportunities to reinforce a positive image of military life to dependant children, who may one day join the service themselves.

A young boy and his father watch a Matador tactical missile streak skyward with its jet-assist rocket ablaze. During Armed Forces Day 1960, this test firing was watched by 4,500 people. Test firings were also centerpiece events during open house air shows in the early 1960s. The Matador missile was tested at Holloman until modifications increased its flying distance beyond the limits of the missile test range.

An aerial overview of Armed Forces Day 1961 shows displays of a GC-130 drone mothership, F-80 Shooting Star chase plane, F-102 Delta Dagger chase plane, B-57 Canberra, and H-21 Shawnee workhorse in the foreground. To the left are the Matador and Mace missiles, two tactical missiles tested extensively at Holloman.

A Q-2 Firebee subsonic missile target and a supersonic XQ-4B are displayed prominently beneath the wing of a GC-130 drone mothership. These were representative examples of the types of drones and remotely piloted vehicles used at Holloman during the early 1960s. In this rare showing at an Air Force open house, an Army RP-76 test vehicle also makes an appearance.

This Armed Forces Day flyover consists of a lead formation of two F-104 Starfighers and two F-100 Super Sabres, followed by a loose diamond formation of four F-106 Delta Darts and four F-84G Thunderjets. All of these models flew for the Air Force Missile Development Center tests, either as missile carriers or chase aircraft.

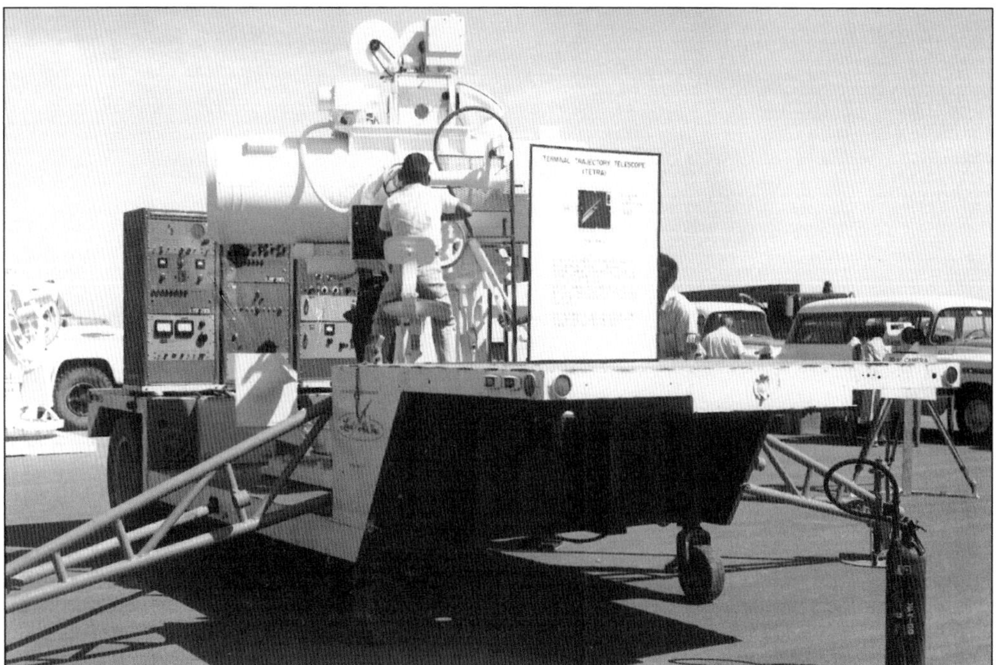

A young boy sits among a static display of the Terminal Trajectory Telescope (TETRA) during the 1961 Open House. TETRA was used to obtain altitude, pitch and roll, time history, and course position data from missile tests. It filmed tests and held more than 53,000 feet of film. Next to the TETRA stand is a comparison 35-mm camera, also used to record tests.

An airman second class walks in front of a Martin Company TM-76 Mace static display during 1961's Open House/Armed Forces Day. The early, or "A," versions of Mace had a range short enough to be tested on Holloman/White Sands Missile Range; the "B" version, however, was tested at the Air Force's open water range at Cape Canaveral, Florida. The first versions of Mace were deployed to Europe in 1961.

Children of the base inspect a missile under the shadow of an F-106 Delta Dart. The military control tower in the background served for many decades, guiding thousands of aircraft over the range and nearby military operating areas in the Sacramento Mountains. Of particular note is the lead boy touching the missile; security restrictions in the current day would not allow the children to see—let alone touch—a missile test article.

Military spouses and young dependants flock to see a working-model section of the 35,000-foot test track during the 1961 Open House/Armed Forces Day program. An example rocket sits in the lower right of the image. The prestige attached to attending an open house is surprising by modern standards. Note the period dresses, fancy footwear, and "Sunday best" worn by the family members.

An F-106 Delta Dart, serial number 56-0464, sits on static display during the annual Armed Forces Day celebration. F-106s were regularly used as chase planes and missile carriers for firing tests. In a twist of irony, F-106s would later return to Holloman's ranges, not as missile carriers, but as missile targets.

An Army H-13 Sioux helicopter painted with a clown face flies past the 1960 Open House crowd. The helicopter and pilot stole the show, entertaining visitors with acrobatic stunts. During the 1970s and 1980s, the H-13 Sioux became easily recognizable to the American public as the helicopter shown during the opening credits of the hit movie and television sitcom *M*A*S*H*.

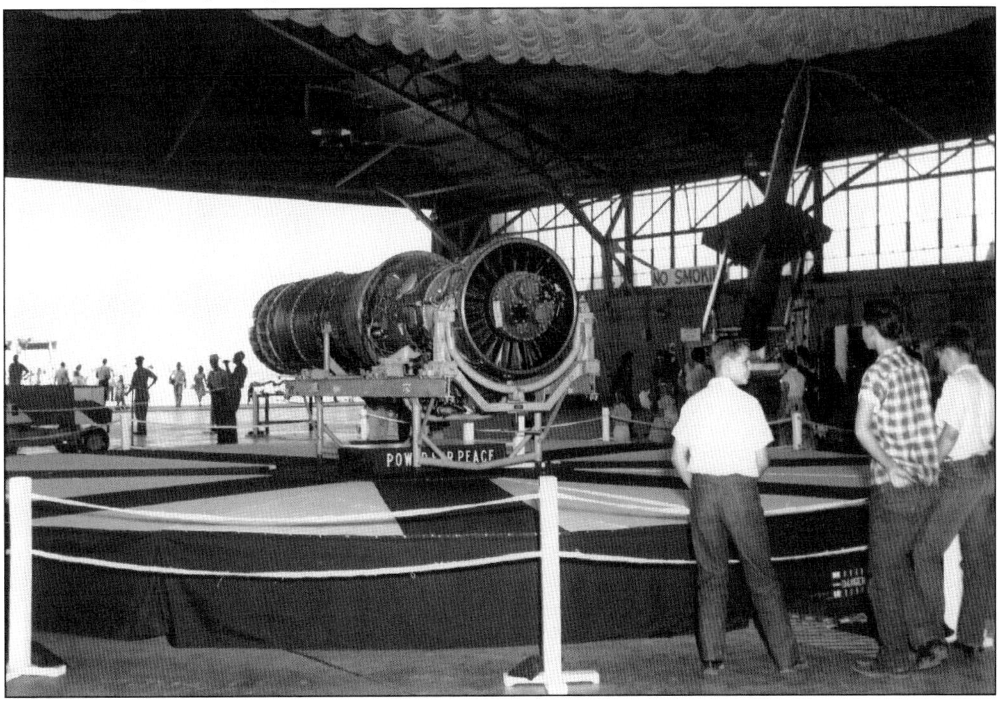

Three young men check out a jet engine on display during the 1961 Open House. The "Power for Peace" label beneath the engine reflected the political atmosphere of the time. The work being done at Holloman—space research and defensive national security measures—was sold to the American public as beneficial to the nation. While true, a side effect of the research was that it allowed for the creation of effective offensive weapons too.

The radio announcer's booth, stationed atop a van with accompanying aerospace ground equipment for power, set up at the 1961 Holloman Open House. Similar setups have been the cornerstone of air shows in decades since. Announcers would describe the approaching aircraft and the names of flight crews while vividly detailing aerial maneuvers. Later shows incorporating flight demonstration teams like the Thunderbirds would have a rock music soundtrack during maneuvers.

TM-76 Mace missiles sit adorning the surrounding desert in a tactical rapid-fire configuration. The Mace was an advanced version of the Matador and the most powerful missile used by Tactical Air Command (TAC). The first versions of the Mace were deployed in 1961 to the 71st Tactical Missile Squadron at Bitburg Airbase, Germany.

A group of visitors clamor over a manned rocket test sled named Sonic Wind No. 2 during the Holloman High Speed Test Track's official opening of the 35,000-foot track on February 25, 1959. This sled succeeded the sled that carried Lt. Col. John P. Stapp to near-Mach speeds on his December 1954 test run.

A 6580th Air Base Group GC-130A, serial number 57-0496, taxis across the runway, showing its wares as a drone-carrying mothership. Underneath the wings on the inner payload pylons are two needle-looking Northrop XQ-4B supersonic target drones. The two outer pylons hold two Ryan Aeronautical Q-2C Firebee drones. The Firebee family of drones stayed active in the US inventory for over 50 years.

A GC-130A drone carrier banks slightly to the left, showing its "passenger," a XQ-4B supersonic target drone, during its first flight in September 1960. After release from the mother aircraft, the sleek XQ-4B drone exceeded Mach 1 without engaging its afterburner. The GC-130's varying light and dark colors were a mixture of white and "safety" orange, distinguishing the aircraft from the drone targets so commonly seen over the test range.

Members of the 366th Tactical Fighter Wing (TFW) and their families exit a C-118 on the Holloman Air Force Base tarmac moments after landing on July 2, 1963. This first flight carried a total of 56 personnel and began the influx of the 366th TFW from France to Holloman. Leading the group was Col. Ralph S. Garman, AFMDC commander (center), and Col. Henry C. Godman, Holloman AFB garrison commander.

Garman's wife hands a freshly baked cookie to one of the newest members of Holloman Air Force Base, making him feel right at home. She and the family service volunteers prepared a base reception for the newly arriving personnel from the 366th TFW after their long journey from France.

At 8:30 a.m on July 2, 1963, local leadership greets C.M.Sgt. Norman Gordon, first member of the 366th Tactical Fighter Wing, off the arriving C-118. Behind Chief Master Sergeant Gordon are, from left to right, Col. Ralph S. Garman, AFMDC commander; Alamogordo mayor Wayne Phelps; and Col. Henry C. Godman, Holloman commander. The aircraft had just arrived with military members and their families from the 366th TFW's previous home in France.

Maj. Felix C. Fowler, operations officer of the 389th Tactical Fighter Squadron, climbs out of his F-84F Thunderstreak. Major Fowler had just finished a 6,400-mile journey from Chaumont Air Base, France, to the new home of the 366th Tactical Fighter Wing at Holloman Air Force Base. Major Fowler had spent time at Alamogordo Army Airfield as a second lieutenant training on B-24 Liberators before taking his 10-man crew to Europe.

A NIKE-Cajun streaks skyward from White Sands Missile Range. The NIKE-Cajun series was the first Air Force missiles to be tested on the Army garrison after a period of the two services' sticking to their "own" ranges. The NIKE-Cajun was, unlike its predecessors, not an air defense missile but a sounding rocket. It could carry a payload of 50 pounds to a height of 120 kilometers.

An OQ-19 aerial target drone is seen here on its launch stand in the late 1950s. Radioplane Company built thousands of OQ-19s for use by many countries' test and target programs. A short-lived variant, the XQ-10, was made mostly of fiberglass and plastic, but it did not enter into widespread production. At the end of the 20th century, more than 73,000 OQ-19 drones had been built.

This photograph details the parachute recovery of an article on the test range. Early rockets at Holloman had sufficient range to get lost in the desert and were of enough monetary and research value that complete recovery was desired. Once the vehicle ran out of fuel, sensors would detect the downward gravity pull and pop out the parachute.

An XQ-1 drone prototype proceeds skyward after launch. The XQ-1 did not gain much favor during its brief time in the Air Force's inventory. Originally designed with a pulse-jet engine, the XQ-1 had a brief endurance time of only 30 minutes. After receiving a turbojet power plant, resultant tests were favorable, but the system lost out to the Ryan Q-2 Firebee series of drones.

An Air Force captain holds a recently retrieved rhesus monkey in front of the shattered remains of an Aerobee test rocket. Between 1951 and 1952, three Aerobee medical flights were performed, with fatal results for the simian passengers on the first two. The third and final flight took two rhesus monkeys to an altitude of 36 miles and brought them back down safely. (Courtesy of the New Mexico Museum of Space History.)

An early Aerobee launch on December 12, 1951, under the designation MX-1011 is shown here. The Aerobee family was a workhorse for the US military and research establishment for nearly 40 years. Over 1,000 rockets were built, and launches supported a variety of activities, including atmospheric research and cosmic ray studies. The first launch of an Aerobee took place on November 24, 1947, and the last launch was completed on January 17, 1985.

T.Sgt. Ben W. McMorron inspects the nosecone of an Aerobee rocket before its 100th launch. The Aerobee required a 60-foot-tall launch tower to maintain rocket stability until the fins could be effective. Aerobee payloads included photographic, solar radiation, biomedical, and atmospheric instruments. Animal passengers onboard Aerobees included small rhesus monkeys and laboratory mice.

Technicians load an Aerobee-Hi sounding rocket through the bottom of the 60-foot launch tower. The Aerobee-Hi program was developed in response to demands for more performance from the basic rocket design. With the additional fuel and longer engine burn time, Aerobee-Hi was able to reach a higher orbital altitude than a standard Aerobee.

Actors Virginia Leith (left foreground) and Martin Milner (right foreground) watch as a test commences at the Holloman Test Track in 1956. The scene was filmed as part of the 20th Century Fox production *On the Threshold of Space*, detailing the country's preparation for conquering outer space. Milner played the role of Air Force lieutenant Morton Glenn, while Leith portrayed a military wife, Pat Hollenbeck.

Film crews for 20th Century Fox complete a scene with Leith and Milner at the high-speed test track for *On the Threshold of Space*. Holloman was a very popular choice for location shooting during the Space Race days and remains so today.

A Bell Aircraft engineer works on MX-776 RASCAL number 2111.

A two-ship formation, with a B-50 and a RASCAL-modified F-80, flies during guidance tests. Note that the nose of the F-80 has the addition of a RASCAL guidance tip attached to the forward fuselage.

Bell Aircraft personnel move a Shrike missile to the loading pit, prior to mating it with a B-50 mothership.

Aerobee test article No. 9 launches on December 12, 1950. While the test was a failure, the early unreliability was engineered out of the Aerobee design, making it one of the most reliable research rockets in the US inventory. Note the height of the Aerobee launch platform, needed to keep the rocket aimed on a straight course skyward for its brief flights.

This panoramic photograph of early Holloman missile pioneers from 1957 features engineers, scientists, and support personnel, including the remaining Operation Paperclip scientists, German engineers from Werner von Braun's V-2 rocket group. The draw of the job and love of rocketry kept the Germans in the basin until the late 1950s, when a mass exodus from Holloman, White Sands, and Fort Bliss moved the greatest minds of rocketry to Huntsville, Alabama.

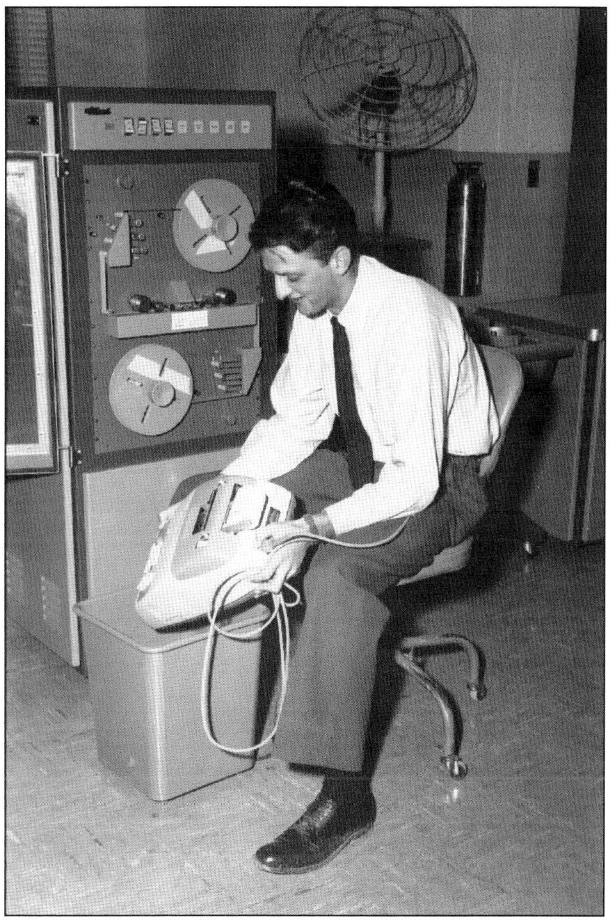

Smiling A1c. Allen Short discards his cumbersome calculator while sitting in front of the Military Pay Branch's new computer. Beginning on January 1, 1964, the Pay Branch began using a mainframe computer to tabulate pay for Holloman personnel. The average pay for an airman first class with over four years experience was $170 per month, barring any other special incentives.

Ferdinand Kuhn receives a professional commendation from Brig. Gen. Leo A. Kiley through Col. Leonard R. Sugarman. Kuhn was part of a follow-up wave of German scientists who arrived at Holloman in 1957. The ethnic mix of the test directorates was heavily German at the start, and although parity was reached with American personnel in the mid-1950s, most chief positions were still held by Germans.

An airborne Mace missile is escorted by T-33s over Holloman airspace in this photograph, taken by an F-100 Super Sabre fighter jet that was also escorting the missile. Giving the F-100 the role of chase aircraft made tactical sense because its varied armament of guns and missiles could shoot down stray missiles or drones, and it had a maximum speed of about 200 miles per hour more than T-33's top speed of approximately 600 miles per hour.

Air Force personnel discuss rocketry tests while leaning on the traveling blockhouse. Given to the 6580th Air Base Group, the mobile blockhouse concept was sound, allowing test directors the same communications they would have at a fixed site. The pyramid structure on top of the blockhouse is the UHF communications antenna used to relay commands to the test article.

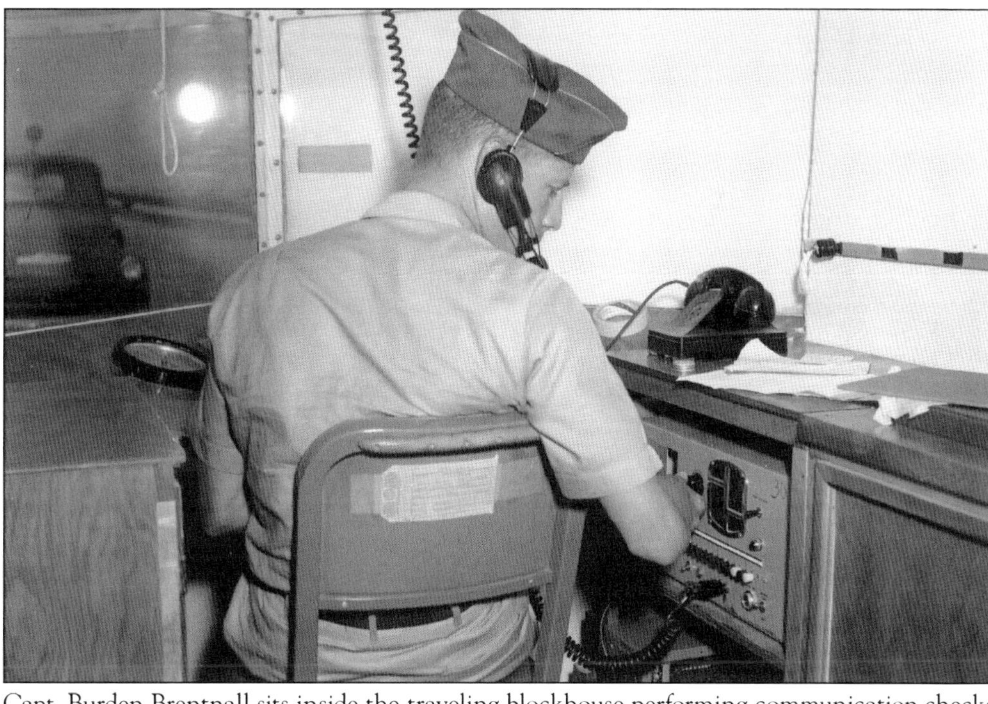

Capt. Burden Brentnall sits inside the traveling blockhouse performing communication checks before a launch. The 1.5-ton structure was moved out on the test range for personnel protection and communications with the airborne observers during a test. The entire structure was created in-house by AFMDC personnel for a fractional cost.

An HH-43B Huskie helicopter tows a facsimile of a Discoverer satellite capsule over White Sands Missile Range in a practice run to demonstrate the feasibility of using helicopters to catch parachute-dropped objects. After the object is snared, the rear compartment winch brings the metal capsule inside the helicopter cabin. Discoverer was the cover story for the military's first photoreconnaissance satellite, Corona.

A rear view of an HH-43B helicopter displays the modifications allowing the rotorcraft to catch parachute-dropped objects in midair. The winch in the rear contains a nylon cable that extends out along two long poles formed into a loop. This apparatus was first used to snare several Discoverer satellite capsules from C-119 and C-130 aircraft.

An HH-43B helicopter makes practice pickups of ground packages of various weights, using its built-in structure for catching parachute-dropped objects. Practice flights are necessary to determine the maneuverability of this type of aircraft for parachute recoveries. Similar winch systems were used on C-130 Hercules aircraft until 1986, when the final film-based reconnaissance satellite mission was launched.

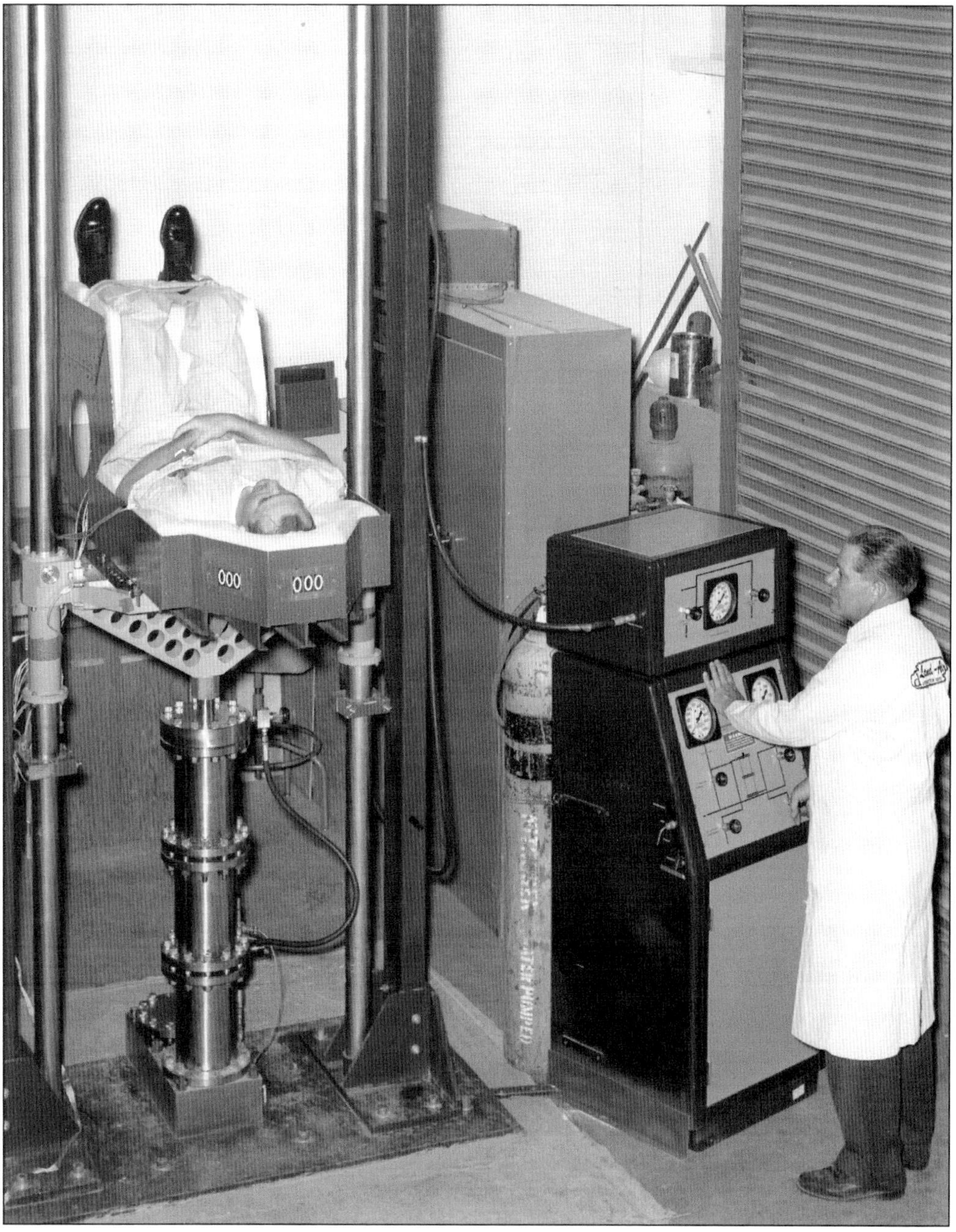

This unique vertical accelerator known as the HYGE ("High-G") shock tester is ready to subject its rider, S.Sgt. Thomas W. Meidl, to a high-G load to determine human physiological effects of acceleration impact. Land-air technician Irving Jacobs stands at the console, ready to actuate the piston that does the accelerating.

Five eminent scientists gather at an American Rocket Society banquet in Alamogordo, New Mexico, during a summer science seminar sponsored by AFMDC. From left to right are Dr. Karl Pohlhausen, Dr. Theodore von Karman, Dr. Paul S. Epstein, Dr. Knox Millsaps, and Dr. Wallace D. Hayes. The summer seminar, with Dr. von Karman as chief lecturer, helped promote the goals of AFMDC's mission as well as Air Force science and research.

Chris Gallegos, shown here, cut the first strand of barbed wire to start construction on Holloman Air Force Base. (Courtesy of the family of Chris Gallegos.)

A TM-76 Mace tactical missile launches at Holloman in this close-up photograph. Tactical cruise missiles were critical during the early years of the Cold War, allowing a flexible deterrent option for the president. With ranges shorter than intercontinental cruise missiles, they had to be stationed within range of their targets—for the Mace, this meant bases in Germany and throughout Europe.

An F-100 Super Sabre flies past four TM-76 Mace-A tactical cruise missiles on Holloman's range. These missiles included an ATRAN radar terrain matching system, which used preprogrammed topographical landmarks to determine flight path. An internal computer compared this route to a prefabricated filmstrip, allowing flight path alterations until the radar image matched the film.

TM-76 Mace serial number 54-3090 sits on its transporter launcher before a test launch. The Mace-A series was similar in basic design to the Matador missile but with a five-foot body length extension. This allowed the vehicle to carry more fuel, extending its range to 800 miles. Additionally, the rocket was carried, fully assembled, on its transporter launcher, with its Mark-28 fusion warhead attached.

A Mace missile departs from its transporter/launcher with the assistance of a rocket engine at full thrust. These tactical missiles were on the literal and figurative forefront of America's nuclear deterrence during the 1950s. Parked within cruising distance of the Soviet Union or its satellite states, a Mace could pack a powerful punch. Its usefulness, however, was limited due to range, preparation, and launch time.

Maj. Gen. Leighton Ira Davis pushes the start button on the inaugural rocket test run down the new, seven-mile-long Holloman High Speed Test Track. General Davis served as commander of Holloman Air Development Center—later redesignated the Air Force Missile Development Center—from September 1954 to July 1958.

Gertrude Davis, the wife of Maj. Gen. Leighton Ira Davis, makes the ceremonial ribbon cut for the grand opening of the Holloman Base nursery. During their time at Holloman, the Davis family was highly involved in community activities.

A Holloman test engineer holds a prototype Hughes YGAR-1 air-to-air missile in 1949. The missile's designation was later changed to AIM-4 FALCON. It was the first operational guided air-to-air missile in the Air Force and entered service in 1956. The final AIM-4 was taken out of the Air Force inventory in 1988 with the retirement of the F-106 Delta Dart.

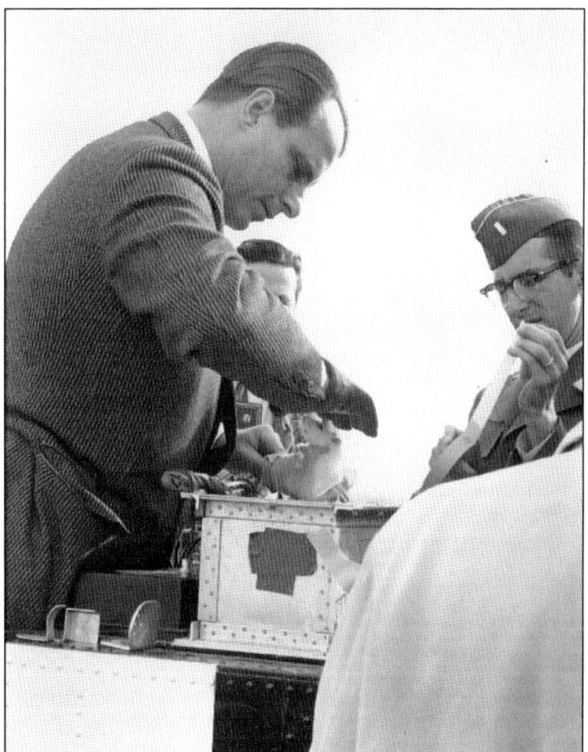

Dr. Harald J. Von Beckh, scientific advisor, and Lt. Albert Zaborowski, task scientist, prepare one of two white rats for their ride on a supersonic sled to test the doctor's new anti-G platform. The test was the opening run on the new 35,000-foot captive missile track at AFMDC.

High school student Ranier Jaenke works at the propellant branch, directorate of advanced technology, AFMDC. The integration of students into Holloman's research work provides dividends for service and community alike. After graduation, the student may see the draw of higher education, and perhaps after college, come back to the base.

Local high school student Mervyn Willard helps out a survey crew at the Area Installation Office. Many civilians who work on the base cite close community ties as a reason to obtain government employment. While it is unknown if Mervyn came back to assist the efforts of Holloman, whether through military or civilian service, many Willards continue to bolster the workforce of the base today.

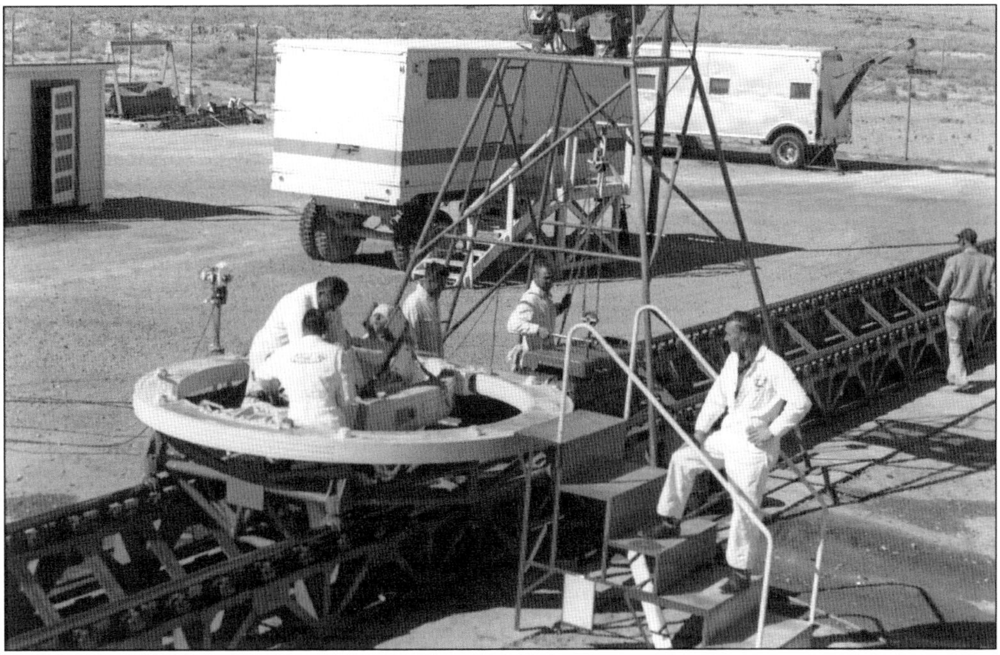

The Daisy Decelerator, a sled-track facility used for biodynamic and equipment impact testing, is seen here in preparation for human-occupied test runs in support of the Apollo program. Operational since 1955, it was developed to produce an impact force capability of up to 200,000 pounds (equivalent to 200 G per 1,000 pounds of total weight), a maximum impact velocity of 175 feet per second.

Holloman personnel help out with firefighting duties during fire season in the Sacramento Mountains, here laboring to curb the fire in the James Canyon and Sixteen Springs area. More than 600 airmen worked side-by-side with Cloudcroft residents and trained Native American firefighters to stem the spread of a costly forest fire that raged in the Lincoln National Forest on May 14–17, 1962.

A B-50 bomber flight crew is seen here before takeoff on a test flight of the XQ-4 drone. From left to right are Northrop test pilots Bill Langstrom and Dale E. Johnson; flight test engineer James E. McCloud; T.Sgts. George Shute, Harry Sappington, and Joseph Boyer; and Lt. John Frishett.

Civil Air Patrol cadets celebrate an anniversary in the late 1950s. From left to right are (first row) Cadets Brunson, Oliver, and Gehlhaar; (second row) Cadets Ortiz, Daunt, Spencer, Stagner, and Spencer. As the USAF Auxiliary, Civil Air Patrol still retains a strong presence in Alamogordo through the present day with Alamogordo Composite Squadron, Wing 073.

This side view shows experiment MX-1601, a sled acceleration/deceleration experiment. Note the three engineers working on the sled bundled inside parkas. While New Mexico is known for high temperatures, occasionally low temperatures combined with high winds necessitate clothing usually seen in Northern locales.

This Radioplane YQ-1B Crossbow configuration is attached to the wing of a B-50 mothership. While seen as a failure by the US Air Force as a target drone, later configurations of the Q-1 would succeed as the GAM-67 Crossbow antiradar missile.

An impacted MX-883 sits after its parachute retrieval on Holloman. The MX-883 was launched from B-29 or B-50 carrier aircraft and was boosted to ignition speed by a single rocket booster attached to the vehicle's tail. The most unusual feature of the MX-883 was its method of recovery. A multistage parachute system slowed the drone to a descent in a vertical nose-down fashion.

Parachutes retrieve an MX-883 drone after it impacted on the range. The performance of the MX-883 proved too advanced for its interceptor missiles; very few hits were scored by the air defense missile crews. Production of the MX-883 series ended in 1959 after 61 airframes had been built.

An experimental rocket is hung under the wing of an F-84F Thunderstreak jet plane. The F-84F was a unique variant of the F-84 Thunderjet design. Designed as a nuclear fighter-bomber, the F-84F was used in a unique capacity by the AFMDC, as a launcher aircraft and also as a chase plane when needed.

An unidentified Navy commander and lieutenant address an Air Force Reserve lieutenant colonel on the characteristics of the naval SAM-N-6 (later renamed RIM-8 Talos) surface-to-air missile, then under test at the White Sands Proving Ground's Land Locked Ship-1 (LLS-1), otherwise known as USS *Desert Ship*. The first of the "T-missiles," the Talos was fired over 500 times on the range during its lifespan.

The Pritch site sits relatively undisturbed among the heat and scrub of the basin. Housing a uniquely designed cinetheodolite tower, the site was used from 1954 through 1973 for range tests. The buildings were constructed to house Askania cinetheodolites, scavenged from Germany after World War II, to record data during V-2 rocket tests. Today, the site remains abandoned on the grounds of Holloman within full view of any interested passerby.

M.Sgt. and Mrs. Ike N. Davis Jr. pose with their son, Thomas Alan, and family dog Fido. M.Sgt. Ike and Mrs. Davis had a combined military service of over 34 years. Davis would eventually be promoted to the highest enlisted rank, chief master sergeant, and fulfill noncommissioned officer in charge (NCOIC) duties at Vandenberg Air Force Base, located on California's Central Coast.

This artist's sketch shows the 260-inch centrifuge built for AFMDC by Genisco, Inc. The 50-foot-diameter structure is equipped with a platform on each end. The centrifuge was built to test systems with up to 116 rotations per minute, producing G-forces as high as 100 Gs. This facility was the most advanced centrifuge in existence during the 1960s.

The enclosure of the Holloman centrifuge was 90 feet in diameter, and the structure stood 24 feet high.

A towering cloud of dust, rubble, bits of hot metal, and desert earth rises over the test track as a monorail rocket sled impacts into a concrete target to test Atomic Energy Commission fusing devices designed for the Army's Pershing missiles. Powered by three 50,000-pound thrust boosters, the sled reached a velocity of 4,328 feet per second—almost five times the speed of a .45 caliber bullet.

This spike monorail sled on Holloman's high-speed test track was a new type designed for greater velocities. Its "flow separation spike" divided the shock wave around the sled to lessen air drag. This design has reached speeds of Mach 5. As of 2012, the speed limit in the great state of New Mexico was still Mach 10.

This 1,200-pound monorail rocket sled with a two-foot-by-two-foot frontal area of solid reinforced concrete hurtles along the test track. Boosted by HI-VAR rockets with a total of 23,200 pounds of thrust and attaining a velocity of 530 feet per second (375 miles per hour), the sled impacted against a 4,500-pound lead and steel barrier fixed to the track. The purpose of the run was impact testing of missile warheads.

This "Mongoose" rocket sled pusher and payload-carrying sled forebody were used in a series of sled run tests during a study of sled separating techniques. The pusher and forebody were separated by blowing apart their couplings with explosive squibs. Separation-included testing improved inertial guidance techniques for warheads in flight.

These narrow-channeled troughs on either side of a rail are effective, when filled with water, at braking monorail sleds because their downward-thrust scoops drag through the water. The braking effect is immediate, with near-Mach high-speed test sleds being brought to zero in only seconds.

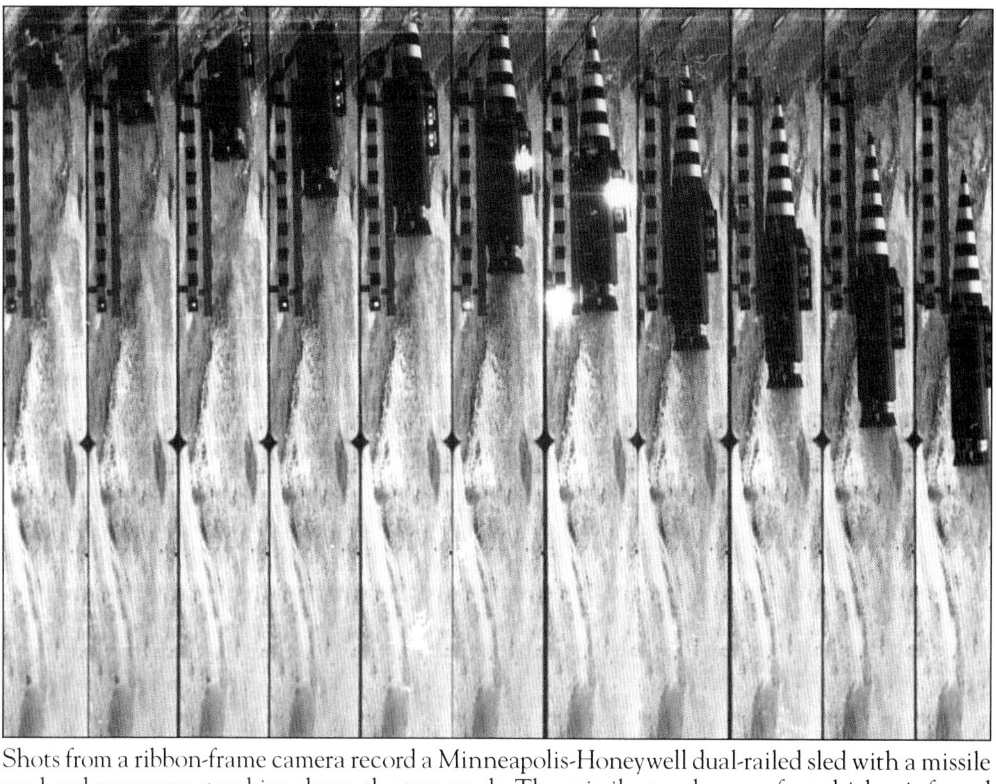

Shots from a ribbon-frame camera record a Minneapolis-Honeywell dual-railed sled with a missile warhead nosecone streaking down the test track. The missile struck a one-foot-thick reinforced concrete target for tests of the warhead's fusing and switching devices. The penetration of the concrete is visible as electronic lights flash and register the correct functioning of switches.

Lt. Howard L. McKinley Jr., chief of the instrumentation development section of the Guidance and Control Directorate, checks out adjustments during test operation of a half-million-dollar test table able to accommodate a complete inertial guidance system. Lieutenant McKinley received an Air Force research and development science award for outstanding work in his field.

A2c. Robert W. Piep (left) and S.Sgt. John E. Flatley calibrate prisms on an improvised optical bench made of nothing but old oil drums and a steel I-beam.

This triple-chambered liquid-engine rocket sled on the test track is used to test inertial guidance systems. Producing 114,000 pounds of thrust, the projectile is fired by combining the deadly duo of red fuming nitric acid and unsymmetrical dimethylhydrazine. This chemical combo has been known since the early days of rocketry to produce high amounts of thrust.

Four

TAC TO THE FUTURE 1970–1990

The diminishing of the tactical missile test mission at Holloman in the late 1960s was driven by political reasons—missiles were increasing in range and sophistication, requiring larger developmental testing areas. Holloman had made quite a splash with its space age research, but that too was drawing to a close due to cutbacks in NASA's manned space exploration programs due to the federal funding of the Vietnam War. While housing the 366th Tactical Fighter Wing (TFW) very briefly in the 1960s, the base took in another fighter unit in 1968, the 49th Tactical Fighter Wing. As the rocket testing and space systems development wound down, the attention on fighter aircraft spun up.

When Air Force Systems Command gave responsibility of the base over to Tactical Air Command on January 1, 1971, the "Fightin' 49ers" took over management of the base and surrounding airspace. The 49th TFW was the Air Force's only dual-based tactical fighter wing, deploying squadrons to Europe to fill NATO commitments while maintaining Holloman as its home station. During the 1972 North Vietnamese invasion of South Vietnam, the entire 49th, except for rear echelon personnel, moved to Takhli Royal Thai Air Force Base to conduct offensive air-to-air operations.

After the war ended, Holloman changed focus to training for Cold War–era combat with the Air Force's newest air superiority fighter, the F-15 Eagle. From the late 1970s through the 1980s, the base held both a tactical fighter wing, the 49th TFW, and a tactical fighter training wing, the 479th TFTW, at the Holloman Tactical Training Center. Undergraduate pilots received fighter-specific training at Lead-In Fighter Training (LIFT), lessening the time needed to train pilots for combat.

The 833rd Air Division took over base-keeping responsibilities from the 49th TFW in 1980 and held them until the end of the Cold War. Holloman aircrews continued to dominate the skies, winning TAC's 1988 William Tell air-to-air competition. Changes in geopolitics at the start of the 1990s oversaw the transition from a garrison force dedicated to fighting the Soviet Union to an expeditionary force, moving airmen all over the world with global reach and global power.

On this early variant of the 49th TFW's logo, the winged knight's helmet reflects the unit's long and distinguished history of military engagements, starting in World War II. The stars represent the Southern Cross, denoting World War II campaign credits in the South Pacific. The lower right corner contains a covered wagon, road, and trees. The 49th's motto remains *Tutor Et Ultor*, "I Protect and Avenge." (Courtesy of the Page Family, New Mexico chapter.)

Holloman personnel stand in formation at a roll call. In continuing historic military traditions, roll call—or muster—is used to determine how many personnel remain with the unit. In ancient times, this would determine how successful the battle was or if replacements for the unit were needed. In modern times, roll call still does this, but it also includes the presentation of awards in front of one's peers.

A security policewoman waves on incoming traffic to the base. Segregation of the sexes continued throughout the first half of the 1970s but was slowly coming to an end. Before this, women took their places among the noncombat roles of the Air Force, as data-entry specialists, medical technicians, or in administrative capacities. On May 31, 1975, Holloman's Women's Air Force (WAF) Squadron Section was phased out.

Three unidentified 49th TFW pilots discuss a sortie. The F-4 Phantom II was a common sight at Holloman during the 1960s and 1970s. The aircraft required a two-person crew, with the pilot in front and the weapons system officer, or "wizzo," sitting in the rear. The various usages of F-4s at the base included delivery aircraft for new missile designs and, in later decades, as a drone aircraft for missile tests.

Facing southwest, this Holloman flight line photograph from around 1968 shows the combined strength of the 7th, 8th, and 9th Tactical Fighter Squadrons. The new arrival of the 49th TFW to Holloman would not be celebrated for long, as the wing would be tasked to exercise the "dual-basing" concept and move over 2,000 personnel and 72 aircraft to Europe for Exercise Crested Cap.

A 49th TFW F-4 Phantom II is directed out of its hardened aircraft shelter during Crested Cap. As part of the US Army's REFORGER (REturn of FORces to GERmany) exercises, Crested Cap proved the viability of moving air assets. In 1972, the 49th earned the MacKay Trophy for the "most meritorious flight of the year," for the redeployment from Germany to Holloman after Crested Cap II. The MacKay Trophy recognized the 49th for the fastest nonstop deployment of jet aircraft accomplished by a wing's entire fleet.

A T-38 flies over the Tularosa Basin, clearly displaying the "HM" tail code of the 479th Tactical Training Wing. The 479th was activated at Holloman on January 1, 1977, to provide LIFT for pilots assigned to fly the McDonnell Douglas F-15 Eagle. Operational tactical fighter training squadrons of the wing (and their tail code stripe colors) were 433rd (black stripe), 434th (red), 435th (blue), and 436th (yellow).

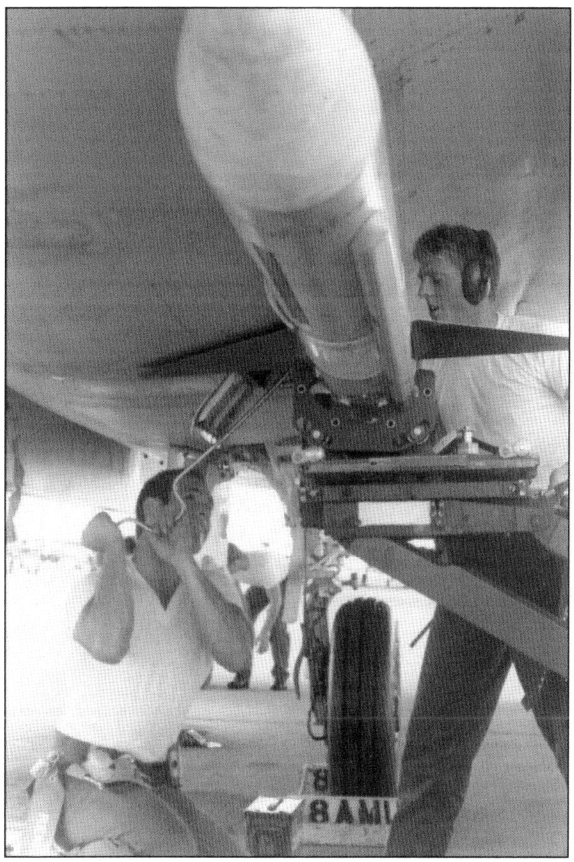

Holloman aircraft armament specialists load an AIM-7 Sparrow air-to-air missile onto an F-15. The F-15's mission of air superiority necessitates the massive armament load the aircraft must carry into combat. With two hard points on each wing, the underside of the F-15 has four fuselage points to carry more missiles. With speed, teeth, and aesthetics, the F-15 has it all.

This Fourth of July parade in downtown Deming, New Mexico, was led by a five-person color guard presentation from Holloman. The surrounding communities in southern New Mexico contain thousands of retired military personnel, and their appearance at formal events, such as parades, cements a positive image of the military with the general public. (Courtesy of the "Steel Talons," Holloman Honor Guard.)

Staff Sergeant Adair, US Air Force Honor Guard, checks his uniform before presentation of the colors. Adair was a member of the 833rd Air Division Honor Guard at Holloman before being hand-selected to represent the entire service as an elite member of the US Air Force Honor Guard in Washington, DC. (Courtesy of the "Steel Talons," Holloman Honor Guard.)

Airman 1st Class Carter's rifle is inspected by an unidentified honor guard sergeant. Members of the 833rd Air Division Honor Guard were forerunners of the present-day Holloman Honor Guard, known as the Steel Talons. The deactivation of the air division and consolidation of the 49th and 479th Wings in the early 1990s forced the renaming of the guard to the "base" honor guard. (Courtesy of the "Steel Talons," Holloman Honor Guard.)

The Consolidated Base Personnel Office, or CBPO, is seen here in the early 1980s. The building still houses support functions such as military personnel flight. Throughout the years, thousands of airmen and their families walked through these doors to obtain new identification cards, check on their pay, or schedule the shipment of their household goods to their next duty station.

A member of the Holloman Honor Guard hands a folded flag to the widow of an American service member. This heart-wrenching duty is one of the solemnest required of honor guard personnel, but is one they perform without reservation. (Courtesy of the "Steel Talons," Holloman Honor Guard.)

Five

Nighthawk Nesting Ground 1990–2000

The dissolution of the Soviet Union in 1991 changed the scope of the Air Force's mission from supporting combat operations in a bipolar world to conducting missions ranging from high-intensity conflict to nonwar operations. During this transition to expeditionary operations, Holloman received a new weapon, the F-117 Nighthawk, better known as the stealth fighter. Fighter pilots changed their tactics too, from facing the enemy in daylight and riding in the world's most capable air superiority fighter to flying missions under the cover of darkness and avoiding all contact with friends and foes alike.

Holloman family members became accustomed to military members spending long periods away from home, and deployment and homecoming ceremonies became regular occurrences on base. While American airmen were extending their global presence, members of the German Luftwaffe began arriving in southern New Mexico, practicing to spread their wings in the swing-wing Tornado fighter.

Test-related activities at Holloman continued throughout the transition out of the Cold War. The 6585th Test Group, the last legacy organization of the Air Force Missile Development Center days, was redesignated the 46th Test Group. Tests continued on the Radar Target Scatter (RATSCAT) range, with the Holloman High Speed Test Track attempting to break the magical number of Mach 10 over land. Projects supported on the range included the ubiquitous Patriot surface-to-air missile system, made famous during the Gulf war, with Holloman engineers operating the MQM-107 Streaker target drone.

At the beginning of the 21st century, great changes were afoot for the base, the fighter wing, and the country as a whole. After the terrorist attacks of September 11, 2001, Holloman personnel were thrust into action—first during Operation Enduring Freedom in Afghanistan and later during Operation Iraqi Freedom in 2003. F-117s flew routinely during the first few weeks of air combat over Iraq, producing "shock and awe" with its stealthy attacks over the capital city of Baghdad.

From the early 1990s through the present day, this has been the emblem of the 49th Fighter Wing. The significance of the logo remains, with the Southern Cross constellation representing the 49th Fighter Group's success in World War II. Missing from the current incarnation is the covered wagon; its original significance is unknown, as are the reasons for its disappearance.

Two F-117As taxi along the runway. The background of the image shows a low-lying tree line, signifying that the stealths were not at Holloman. The popularity of the fighter's public image after Desert Storm was evident with its numerous air show appearances around the world. The appearances took a toll on the fleet, with one, serial 81-793, disintegrating in mid-air during a show in Maryland on September 14, 1997.

Three 49th FW personnel line up for anthrax shots at an undisclosed location in the Middle East. US military activity in the Middle East increased after the 1991 Gulf War, and by extension, the tempo of operations at Holloman increased as well. Transitioning from a TAC fighter base to a bustling Air Combat Command base with worldwide commitments was a welcome change for some Holloman residents.

Maintenance members of the 9th Fighter Squadron, the "Flying Knights," have an impromptu meeting on the flight line of an undisclosed location in the Middle East.

The commander of the 49th Fighter Wing, Col. James P. Hunt, wishes good luck to an unidentified captain in the 8th Fighter Squadron, the "Black Sheep." Colonel Hunt, Bandit No. 384, is an experienced F-117A pilot, beginning his stint with the plane in 1991. After leading the Black Sheep as squadron commander in 1993, he returned to the Fightin' 49ers in 2002 as wing commander.

Colonel Hunt, back as commander of the 49th Fighter Wing, returns an enthusiastic salute from an unidentified senior airman. The aircraft in the background, a contracted Delta Airlines jet, became a familiar sight to the New Mexico skies in the last few decades. To avoid using fuel-guzzling military aircraft to ship personnel overseas, the Department of Defense contracted commercial jets to ship squadrons and their gear to their end destinations.

This top view shows an F-117A over the Sacramento Mountains. The key to stealth was discovered inside a Soviet technical journal by a Lockheed engineer in the early 1970s, The paper, written by Russian physicist Pyotr Ufimtsev in 1962, was titled "Method of Edge Waves in the Physical Theory of Diffraction." Ironically, because the work was considered of no military or economic value, it was allowed to be published internationally.

A group of Holloman personnel enjoy a meal at an undisclosed location in the Middle East. When deployed, mealtime heightens awareness of one's surroundings, so the amenities of home are ever-present. Every holiday was celebrated with gusto, with decorations and greeting cards from appreciative Americans placed on any available wall space.

A Nighthawk pilot escorts his family down the crew access ladder after a peek inside an F-117.

An F-117 is assembled in Burbank, California. While conspiracy theorists have postulated that the Nighthawk contains UFO technology, this photograph shows it is a man-made creation of aluminum, steel, and titanium. The angular facets of the aircraft's body can clearly be seen, though that is not the only part to the stealth equation. The addition of radar-absorbing material to the aircraft's skin helps it to remain "low observable" on radar. (Courtesy of Lockheed Aircraft.)

Members of the 8th Fighter Squadron, the "Black Sheep," show their pride in country, unit, and base. In World War II, while the 7th and 9th Squadrons received new aircraft, the 8th received their hand-me-downs. Unhappy with being last on the supply line, and disapproving of the unlucky "Eightballs," the pilots began calling the 8th "the Black Sheep" Squadron.

Members of the 49th Maintenance Group stand at parade rest before the departure of Nighthawks on an indeterminate deployment.

Two senior airmen engage in an intimate moment prior to departure from Holloman.

The logo of the 20th Fighter Squadron, the "Silver Lobos," adorns the wall of Holloman's Heritage Center. The 20th FS trained German air force pilots and weapon system operators in support of US/German foreign military sales agreements. The presence of the German air force at Holloman began in 1992 with F-4 instruction but increased to include flight training with its Tornado strike aircraft.

The "HO" tail code is prominently displayed on three F-4Es flown by the 20th Fighter Squadron. The quirky humor of ground crews is legible on the left and center aircraft's tail flashes near the top, with serial 72-174 stating "3rd I Blind," after the popular 1990s music group Third Eye Blind, and the left hand aircraft is nicknamed "The Dud."

This F-15A, designated "City of Alamogordo," is displayed at the Holloman Heritage Air Park. While Holloman's 49th Wing flies the F-15's successor, the F-22A Raptor, Eagles still provide top cover for the United States. Since the Raptor was not produced in large numbers, the F-15 will remain in the Air Force's inventory for the foreseeable future.

Located in the base's heritage airpark, this F-117A retains the name of Maj. Greg Feest, call sign "Beast," who was the first Nighthawk pilot to enter Iraqi airspace during 1991's Operation Desert Storm. Now a major general, Feest is the most experienced Nighthawk pilot. He was the first to fly 1,000 hours in the craft, and he holds the most combat hours, rumored to be around 130. Major General Feest first starting flying the F-117 in 1988 and was given Bandit No. 261.

Just as every aircraft has a serial number (designated by the year and production number on the tail), all F-117 pilots who have qualified on the aircraft have earned a "Bandit" number, designated by the day, month, and year they earned it. With the aircraft's retirement in 2008, the numbers are fixed and recorded for posterity inside the Holloman Heritage Center, just outside the airpark, which is the home of F-117A serial 85-816.

An AT-38B prepares for takeoff. After the cessation of the LIFT program during the mid-1990s, the AT-38Bs were furnished as training aircraft for the 49th FW pilots, and as test aircraft for the 586th Flight Test Squadron. As flight hours on F-117As can run into the thousands of dollars per hour, time on smaller aircraft costs a lot less but still provides needed flying experience time.

The raven tail of AT-38B, serial 65-373, is contrasted against the setting sun. The tail flash denotes F-117A silhouettes, showing that T-38s were often used for training F-117A pilots. The T-38s remain at Holloman, even after the retirement of the stealth fighter, due to the arrival of the F-22A Raptor, whose flying costs match or exceed the amount needed for the F-117A.

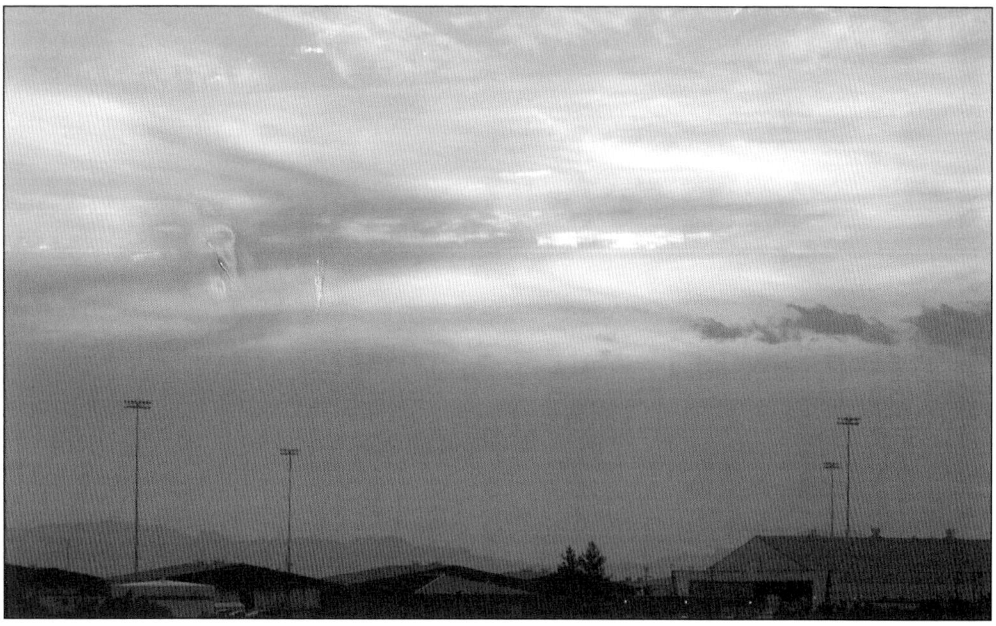

The sun sets on the New Mexico skies, preparing pilots for night missions in the clear evening air. Flying activities at Holloman did not just take place during sunlit hours. After the arrival of the F-117 in New Mexico, it was routine for pilots to fly nighttime sorties over Albuquerque and other Southwestern cities, "bombing" specific locations by identifying buildings on their nighttime scopes.

An unidentified senior airman talks with George House (right). As curator of the New Mexico Museum of Space History, House received stewardship of many test articles from Holloman's space research days. The museum, located in the foothills of the Sacramento Mountains on Alamogordo's eastern edge, showcases many items from the early days of the Space Race.

Remnants of Holloman historical hardware line the New Mexico Museum of Space History's storage lot in Alamogordo.

A member of the 48th Rescue Squadron (RQS) stands next to his MH-60 Pave Hawk helicopter. Para-rescue jumpers (PJs) of the 48th RQS called Holloman home from 1993 through 1999. The varied terrain surrounding the base, with desert and mountains, offered PJs a good environment to practice their craft, as did frequent lost hikers in need of rescue.

Visitors cluster around the edges of F-117 Nighthawk serial number 85-836 on static display during the 1995 Holloman Open House. The aircraft, named "Christine," after the Stephen King novel, flew 39 missions during the Gulf War. Off-center in this photograph, a "restricted area" sign informs visitors that even during an air show, the cordoned area around the plane required strict security, subject to lethal enforcement. (Courtesy of the Page Family, New Mexico chapter.)

The Boeing B-52 Stratofortress makes a rare appearance during an air show at Holloman. B-52s came from Barksdale Air Force Base, Louisiana, and were a popular attraction. In the afternoon hours, the overhead sun would drive many visitors under the shady wings of the B-52 or other large aircraft. Historic Hangar 301 can be seen on the right. (Courtesy of the Page Family, New Mexico chapter.)

The F-117A gets a nose-on view during the 1995 Holloman Air Show. Even with its stealth technology being over 15 years old, public showings of the F-117 required stringent security measures, noted by the "entry point" sign and armed guard. The static display also showcased the F-117's "teeth"—a GBU-27 Paveway III laser-guided bomb. (Courtesy of the Page Family, New Mexico chapter.)

A US Army aviation branch UH-60 Blackhawk provides air show visitors a place to climb and rest their weary feet during the 1995 Holloman Air Show. The Army garrisons at White Sands and Fort Bliss, Texas, had rotorcraft such as the UH-60 to support maneuver forces. Holloman also houses Army aviation assets to support a variety of range activities. (Courtesy of the Page Family, New Mexico chapter.)

An F-4F Phantom II, with its tail flash clad in German air force colors, sits on the tarmac during the 1995 Holloman Open House. When the German air force arrived at Holloman in 1992, the US Air Force's 20th Fighter Squadron was tasked with training Luftwaffe pilots and weapon systems officers, initially using the F-4 airframe and later utilizing the Panavia Tornado strike aircraft. (Courtesy of the Page Family, New Mexico chapter.)

Family members of "Team Holloman" arrive to greet their safely returned loved ones. During the 1990s and early 2000s, Holloman members were deployed in various locations around the globe. The time deployed varied from 60 days up to one year, but the feeling of relief and excitement among families when their loved ones arrived home was universal, regardless of the time deployed.

Technical Sergeant Munroe performs a sharp salute for departing F-117s. The romantic legends of the salute claim that the military tradition began in the days of chivalry. Approaching knights would lift their visors with their weapon hand, verifying their identity and that they were unarmed. Whatever the origin, the tradition of the salute has continued to the present day as a sign of respect between comrades.

Holloman's missile tests are still an active part of the base's mission. Here, a Soviet-era MAZ-543 transporter/erector/launcher (TEL), complete with SS-1 Scud missile, is transported on an open New Mexico highway. Throughout the 1990s, Exercise Roving Sands incorporated Army air defense crews with Air Force aircraft and "other" participants (such as the Scud TEL) to test a live, threatening air defense environment in the southern New Mexico desert.

Members of the 49th Aeromedical Dental Operations and 49th Medical Dental Operations Squadrons complete final assembly of a chemical warfare treatment tent in the exercise area during Holloman Air Force Base's Phase II Exercise. (US Air Force photograph by S.Sgt. Ken Lustig.)

The author kneels before the Holloman base sign in 1997. The lull in mainstream operations during the early 1990s and change of focus towards humanitarian operations did not lessen Holloman's operations tempo. Being the lone operational base for the stealth fighter force increased Holloman's visibility in the press, especially during Operation Allied Force, when one F-117 was shot down over Kosovo by the Serbian army. (Courtesy of the Page Family, New Mexico chapter.)

BIBLIOGRAPHY

Cooper, Sonya and Jean Fulton. *"Full Moral and Material Strength": The Early Cold War Architectural Legacy at Holloman Air Force Base (ca. 1950–1960).* Holloman AFB, NM: 49th Civil Engineer Squadron, 1996.

Gibson, James N. *Nuclear Weapons of the United States: An Illustrated History.* Atglen, PA: Schiffer Publishing, Ltd, 1996.

Hawthorne, Lori S. *I Never Left a Place That I Didn't Clean Up: The Legacy of Historic Settlement on Lands Administered by Holloman Air Force Base.* Holloman AFB, NM: 49th Civil Engineer Squadron, 1994.

Hawthorne-Tagg, Lori S. *A Life Like No Other: Ranch Life on Lands Now Administered by Holloman Air Force Base.* Holloman AFB, NM: 49th Civil Engineer Squadron, 1997

Mattson, Wayne O. and Martyn D. Tagg. *"We Develop Missiles, Not Air!": The Legacy of Early Missile, Rocket, Instrumentation, and Aeromedical Research Development at Holloman Air Force Base.* Holloman AFB, NM: 49th Civil Engineer Squadron, 1995.

Meeter, George F. *The Holloman Story.* Albuquerque: University of New Mexico Press, 1967.

Mueller, Robert. *Air Force Bases, Volume I: Active Air Force Bases within the United States of America on 17 September 1982.* Washington, DC: Office of Air Force History, 1989.

Weitze, Karen J. *Guided Missiles at Holloman Air Force Base: Test Programs of the United States Air Force in Southern New Mexico, 1947–1970.* Holloman AFB, NM: 49th Civil Engineer Squadron, 1994.